U. A. W.'s
FRONTIER

JAMES D. HILL, AUTHOR
Copyright© 1971 by U.A.W. Region 3 Auto Council
All rights reserved,
Library of Congress Catalog Number 76-152491

Second Printing
February, 1976
Published By
U.A.W. Region 3
Dallas Sells, Director

Mr. and Mrs. Walter P. Reuther are shown above at the 20th Anniversary Celebration of the U.A.W. at South Bend, Indiana in 1956.

WE WISH to express our gratitude to the many people who aided us in our efforts. To Jim Poland, Pete Ruppert, Ed Wygant and Jack Richards of Local No. 9 for their interest and cooperation.

To all of the Local No. 5 members who furnished information, advice, and pictures. To Dolores Romeu and Hazel Bennett of the U.A.W. Mishawaka office for their many assists over and beyond the call of duty.

To Peggy Flora and Lavina Schwind for their patient and expert typing from the author's atrociously hand written pages.

To Don Ballard of the Region 3 staff for his professional skill and cooperation with the photography and book layout.

To my wife for her patience, understanding, and inspiration.

The Author

PREFACE

The story of Organized Labor in the United States prior to the Big Depression is a sad chapter in our history. Few, if any of the governments of other free countries had allowed such exploitation of employees by their employers in modern times.

The Big Business control of news media had created an image of employers as heroes and unions as villains. The writers and publishers who dared champion Labor's cause became victims of the black ball and advertising starve-outs.

Merchants, manufacturers, and the majority of the educators and politicians collaborated to brand unions of factory workers as foreign and subversive. Such was the majority attitude when the Big Depression struck. Even the majority of industrial workers shared the attitude and many retained it throughout the depression.

There were however, many people in all walks of life whose eyes had been opened to the perfidy of the counterfeit opinion makers. The blind greed and outright stupidity of the controlling business magnates and ruling politicians had greatly diminished the Hero Image. Their ineptitude and impotency under stress was the disgrace of the century.

President Roosevelt's seeds of advice to workers found many fertile spots among the thorns and stones of our anti-union oriented soil. One of the most amazing enigmas of history however, is that so many of their abused victims still worshiped the employers' brazen images.

In our story we deal mainly with the labor people of South Bend and the events that happened there. With a few exceptions the period covered is from 1933 to 1953. The main stress is on 1933 through 1940 because those were UAW's most formative and critical years.

The fact that we dwell so much on Locals No. 5 and 9 is based on two reasons. Number one is that they were the only actually fully organized operating Locals for the first three or four years. The second and main reason was the lack of facts due to the almost impossible task of record keeping by the smaller Locals in the earlier days.

The "action" pictures of varied union events is a tiny sampling of the activities and functions. It is the hope of the author they will help portray the character and caliber of the UAW movement.

The pictures of the people involved are mainly those who were active union warriors during the 1933 to 1943 era. This too is only a small sampling. The attrition of time, archaic record facilities, and the writer's inability to get responses leaves out many who made great contributions.

If some of the picture captions sound like eulogies such has been well earned and it is so intended.

James D. Hill

TO THE FRONTIERSMAN

IT IS a sad fact of history that openers of frontiers far too seldom get to share in their richest harvests. Such, however, was not the case of UAW's frontiersmen.

True, not all survived to enjoy the big wage and working condition improvements. Company paid Pensions, Health and Welfare Plans, and most of the other big contractual gains came too late for many.

To the pioneers though went the richest of rewards of a substance and a quality far beyond any money value. A whole class of people broke out of serfdom into full citizenship. Their wistful and furtive dreams of human dignity became a reality. The workers in South Bend started vigorously to tear down the walls of race, creed and color prejudice. The generation-old barriers of the many ethnic enclaves started to dissolve. The catalyst was the amalgam of brotherhood.

The feeling of camaraderie born of fighting the good fight for a great cause has more enduring value than gold. To have walked in their ranks and shared their defeats and victories was a privilege beyond compare.

Such treasures moth and rust cannot corrupt.

EXIST

CHAPTER 1

THE ROARING TWENTIES

THIS VOLUME will not attempt to cover the vast area of the conflicts, the attitudes, and the chaotic conditions during the Big Depression of the early 1930's. However, since our subject, Industrial Unionism, had its genesis during, and because of, the depression we must touch upon some of the history of that period.

The Roaring Twenties was an era of big action. Big spending, big gambling, big debts, in fact, big everything existed to a point of folly beyond any since the fall of the Roman Empire.

Speculators were the glamour symbols of rich and poor, of youth and age. Rent and grocery money, college tuition, trust funds, life savings, money from every available source went into the action. Stock markets, grain pits, real estate deals, and myriads of other get-rich-quick meccas vied for the millionaires' plenty and the peasants' pittance.

The atmosphere of quick and easy money attracted confidence men and professional gamblers from all corners of the world. Wildcat oil wells, watered stock, fictitious gold and silver mines, and similar swindles robbed both the rich and the poor.

Many appeals for government controls were made by those who were informed as to the ways of finance. Economists and bankers, churches and labor unions warned of disaster if the orgies of speculation weren't controlled. The monetary systems of the world were being endangered by the fiscal irresponsibility of reckless financial manipulation.

Small minorities in both Houses of Congress attempted to introduce corrective measures but the majority of Congressmen and the National Administration refused to cooperate. They contended that free enterprise needed no controls, and that the economy had never been more sound.

Even after the colossal stock market crash on "Black Friday," October 29, 1929, the leaders of the Federal and most of the State governments refused to take any action to lessen the shock or to protect the ruined victims of those unscrupulous manipulators of finance.

Many who had gambled away their own and the savings of their friends and clients committed suicide while others ended up in mental institutions. The very rich got richer and the poor became poorer with hordes of new paupers added to their already swollen ranks.

South Bend was an important manufacturing center and its products were known over all the world. It was the home of the oldest then existing makers of transportation vehicles, cast iron plows, and sewing machines. Studebaker, Olivers and Singers had been the mainstays of the community for several generations. Fathers, sons, and grandsons often worked side by side in the plants and many lived within walking distance in the same neighborhoods.

It was considered a good city to live in, and to work in. There were almost no slums, such as existed in all of the larger cities and in too many of the smaller ones throughout the rest of the country. During the 1920's new industries moved in — old ones expanded — and, employment increased by leaps and bounds. Except for a brief recession in the spring of 1924 it was a bounteous era for South Bend industry.

Mid-west agriculture and coal mining however had not enjoyed the benefits of the lush times. Farmers were on the bottom of the profit graphs almost every year. The mid-west coal miners only worked from fifty to seventy-five percent of the time.

The propserous times in South Bend beckoned to thousands of impoverished farmers and miners. People came from not only the mid-west, but from some of the far western areas and from the south.

AUTO AGE BEGINS

The first couple of decades of the 20th Century had seen the automobile grow from a joke and conversation item to a revolution in America's traveling habits. Hundreds of auto companies had sprung up around the country but the majority of them were already out of business by 1920.

A new industry had been born and with it hundreds of new skills and thousands of new jobs. As the horseless carriage progressed farther and farther from its horse drawn forerunner so did the techniques of manufacture and distribution.

Working in an automotive plant in the 1920's was interesting and often exciting. The industry was emerging from the handcraft methods of production into the specialized techniques of mass production. Conveyor lines replaced the stationary benches and work tables and power tools began the take-over from many of the hand tools of the craftsmen.

Highly skilled production trades that had taken years to learn were broken down into many less complicated operations that could be learned in a matter of months or, in some instances, in a few days.

Skilled automobile craftsmen such as metal finishers, torch solderers, trimmers, painters, hammer-men, and cloth cutters were in high demand throughout the industry. Many of them made a practice of following the boom times from shop to shop. Flint, Grand Rapids, Milwaukee, Toledo, Detroit, and South Bend were all on the "floaters" routes as they followed the "big money" around the country.

The exchange of gossip between these itinerants was a never ending source of interest. Some of them had been members of groups that attempted to organize unions in various plants. Several were in the drives of the IWW (Industrial Workers of the World) in their brief but hectic contests with the copper and silver mine owners of Montana, Wyoming, and Colorado. Others had been through the strikes and starve-outs of the coal mines of Kentucky, Indiana, and Illinois.

Their experiences had a strong influence on the workers who felt that unions should be organized for auto workers.

As the depression became more severe this feeling about unions increased but the very mention of it was to risk immediate firing.

Management attitudes and personnel policies varied widely. This was often true within the various shops of the same Company. Some divisions and departments were fairly and honestly administered, while others were ruled by tyrants and demagogues.

Petty racketeering by a few of the supervisors flourished in certain areas of most shops. The rigged raffle was a favorite technique and a most lucrative one. It was not uncommon to see the same identical "prize" raffled off within a period of two or three months in a half-dozen widely scattered areas of a large plant.

Piece workers who kicked back a bit of tribute to the boss always drew the better priced jobs. The men who painted the boss's house worked the extra hours. After the unions became strong enough to provide adequate protection the stories began to be told. Example: A department foreman stopped at an employee's home in the country and expressed admiration for his fat pigs. In due time, one of the pigs, all dressed and cut up, was delivered to said foreman's house as a "friendly gift."

All through the slack winter of 1931-32 the donor worked 40 or more hours per week while the majority worked less than 15 hours weekly. Hogs were bringing from 6 to 8 cents a pound at the market but he estimated that one netted him $3.00 per pound!

Nepotism generally determined who got the choice jobs. Apprenticeships went to the sons, grandsons, and nephews of foremen and superintendents. It generally was who one knew rather than what one knew.

During the early twenties a majority of the industries in South Bend had a practice of working 55 hours per week. This generally consisted of five days at ten hours and five hours on Saturday.

The practice, however, didn't apply if more hours were necessary or if work was slack and less hours were required. None of the companies went to much bother about giving prior notice when the work hours were to be changed. It was on a day to day basis with notice given about an

4

hour before regular quitting time. If someone had plans for the next day and inquired about the likelihood of working late he was curtly told to wait and see.

The hours could be different between departments and often within the same department. Ride pools were almost impossible to maintain and many a worker had to hitch hike for miles.

One of the most intolerable conditions resulted from a petty racket operated by some supervisors. Most production workers were on piece work while supervisors and inspectors were on a flat hourly rate, often earning only 75% to 80% of the amount the piece worker earned.

In areas where it could be worked supervisors collaborated with inspectors to hold back approval on a sizable portion of the work ordinarily done during the regular day. Just before quitting time they would serve notice that the group must work until 9:00 or 10:00 o'clock at night. Thus the day workers got an additional four or five hours pay while the piece worker had to stay the extra time just to get the amount he normally made in a regular day.

In the mid-Twenties some effort was made to reduce the work week to 45 hours but many employees still worked up to 75 hours while others got 40 or less. There was no such thing as time and one-half pay or night shift premium. The big weeks were, more often than not, awarded as patronage based upon who you were, not what you could do.

When the depression came there were many days when workers were told to come in but no work was available. After waiting around for hours they would be sent home with orders to report the next day and the same process repeated itself, often for four or five days in succession.

Whenever a worker objected to such a waste of his time he was reminded that thousands of people would be glad to take his place in the waiting line.

Petty rackets were operated in those situations also. Employees who were willing to pay a tribute to the boss left the shop with the others but sometimes a half hour or so later would slip back in. They often worked enough hours to make up a full week while the others got no work at all.

Each supervisor that practiced these nefarious schemes maintained a spy system to protect his interests.

If a wave of protest against his racketeering started to roll too high, the leaders of the revolt would get word to lay-off or else. The "else" might be sugar in the gas tank, a roughing-up or discharge on a trumped up pretext.

The rank and file workers detested the willing stooges even worse than the crooked supervisors. They were given many titles; most of them unprintable, but an old World War I vet dubbed them the Red Apple Corps which title most aptly fitted.

CHAPTER 2

THE BIG DEPRESSION

THE FIRST shock waves of the Depression didn't immediately bother many of South Bend's factory workers too seriously. That would come a little later, but many speculators, especially those in home construction who had stretched their resources too thin were wiped out over night and this seriously, and instantly, affected construction employment and related industries.

Depressions or "panics" were no novelty in the early decades of the 20th Century. Economic slumps of varying degree of severity had been occurring at four to eight year intervals as far back as anyone could remember.

The winter of 1929-30 was slow but not unusually bad for employment in South Bend factories, however other segments of industry had suffered sharply.

Optimistic financial experts forecast that with the coming of Spring all would be well—but, the jolt had been too great and prosperity didn't come back with the birds and the flowers.

Layoffs and short hours marked the summer of 1930 and by the year's end wage cuts had been made in several plants. Many of those that had migrated in for the booming times now had to pack up and try to get back home. Too many had no place to return to. Their plight was desperate because many had not established sufficient tenure of residence to qualify for county relief.

Shack towns, generally referred to as "Hoovervilles" began to spring up around the edges of South Bend. Sometimes as many as ten people would live in a one-room shack only fifteen by twenty feet in size. The occupants had to endure no plumbing, often no water, and, only the crudest means of cooking and heating.

In some of the older areas of the city itself, slum conditions began to grow for the first time. People with very little shared their misery with others who had nothing.

Violent crime increased manifold in every category but especially in holdups and burglaries. Live stock rustling made a reappearance after decades of absence. Automobile theft, often for the stripping of tires and batteries, became a way of life for some of the jobless and desperate men.

Job seekers without a dollar travelled from state to state equipped only with their nerve and a siphon hose. Their philosophy of comfort was that, if caught, jail food was far better than none.

1931 in South Bend brought more wage cuts, more layoffs, and hardships of many complexities.

A substantial portion of the population was deep in debt. Homes, cars, furniture, and many other items had been bought in the easy times of prosperity but now poverty was in season. With few customers for repossessed items many merchants took the route of garnishment to add still more misery to already unbearable loads of debts.

Many a citizen with eight or ten years of equity in a home saw similar homes selling for less than he still owed on his. Banks that foreclosed and couldn't resell were stuck with much of their cash tied up in non-saleable, non-interest bearing collateral. Bank failures became a common occurrence and all too often resulted in ruinous losses by the depositors.

By fall of 1931 people began to default on personal and property taxes until there was genuine alarm that the city and county governments might be without enough funds to operate. At the same time more and more citizens had to ask county aid for food, fuel, medicine, and often for clothing and housing.

The dole lines became so long that people were issued numbers with the time and date to appear for their allotments. The quantity and the quality of the goods received were generally poor but the recipients had no one to adjust a complaint.

The Studebaker management set up commissaries and sold food and fuel to their employees on credit thus allowing many of them to avoid the dole lines. They also aided employees in planting gardens on nearby truck farms. Much of their produce was canned for winter consumption.

Adamant Refusal By Government

The demand for State and Federal intervention to slow the downward dive of the plummeting economy became greater every month. Citizens from every walk of life, many who earlier had been bitterly opposed to such a course now clamored for government aid.

Even though many members of Congress now saw the need, the President made no meaningful effort to initiate programs of alleviation for the daily worsening situation. His advisors still forecast that the economy would bounce back just as it always had before and that a renewed era of prosperity was just around the corner. He finally proposed a "Public Works Program" that consisted of building a couple of hundred postoffices around the entire country. This provided a few months of employment for possibly 100,000 men.

The only public works building program of any consequence was in Washington D.C. where unemployment was the lowest due to most citizens there holding Federal jobs.

High import tariffs that had been enacted in 1930 by a Republican Congress prompted retaliation by 33 of the country's best foreign nation customers. They adopted equally high trade barriers that almost ended the once heavy trade between Europe and Asia and the United States.

This was an especially hard blow in South Bend where Bendix, Oliver, Singer and Studebaker had depended heavily on their exports. The obvious result followed: more layoffs, more wage cuts and, more people on already over-loaded county relief.

The States, counties and municipalities, desperate for help, petitioned to the President for a Federally financed relief system. He told his petitioners that he was still un-

9

alterably opposed to any type of dole either direct or indirect, and that poor relief was not a Federal responsibility.

With the coming of 1932 conditions grew steadily worse.

In many shops the wage rates had been cut one-half, or more, from the 1929 level and very few employees worked half of the time. In the largest plant in town, Studebaker, the average hourly wage was down about sixty percent and the working hours by about the same percentage.

As the financial cirsis deepened, some of the oldest banks in the area were forced to close and thus wiped out, or tied up, the savings of many who had no other resources. This was an era of despair and suicides, and, out of it grew an overwhelming wave of distrust and rebellion. Its target were the men in high finance whose excesses and arrogant disregard for the consequences had destroyed the hopes of so many.

In Washington an impotent and unwilling Administration continued to promise that "prosperity was Just Around the Corner."

DEPRESSION DEEPENS

One of the first segments of the population to suffer from the grinding poverty of the Big Depression was the American farmer. His lot had been hard for more than a decade before 1930 but it plunged to a new low then. Corn dropped to fifteen cents a bushel — it cost at least twenty cents to produce and that without counting the farmers' wages.

Hogs dropped to six cents live weight — and in some areas there were no takers for three cents a pound. Beef and dairy product prices suffered almost as much and poultry often cost more to feed than the income they brought in.

In face of all this plenty and the ruinously low prices millions of people went to bed hungry every night. It was felt first and hardest in the big cities but by 1931 South Bend people by the thousand were hungry most of the time. Township trustees handled county relief in most cases as fairly as they could but even their low quality and meager allotments were denied to many ineligible. Others who were

10

eligible were too proud to "live off the county" and chose to go hungry instead.

From 1931 on it was common for many men to bring nothing or almost nothing for lunch. They didn't talk about it then but later it was explained they had to make a choice of fasting themselves or see their children go with nothing.

The winter of 1931-1932 was colder—in many homes —than most of that generation had ever known before. Men, women and little children patrolled the railroads daily for the few lumps of coal to be found. Some sympathetic railroaders caused extra lumps to fall and often looked the other way when some daring "gleaner" hopped a slow moving coal car.

Studebaker loaned trucks to enterprising employees who went out to the farm wood lots and cut wood on a share basis with the owners. Too many, however, weren't able to take advantage of any of these unusual practices and they often went to bed cold.

By autumn of 1932 the downward speed of the economy had reached a frightening rate. Businesses of long standing and great reputation were going bankrupt every day, hundreds of banks had closed that year, and people with savings still intact, were putting them in hiding.

A third of the working population was totally unemployed and another third was working less than one half time at less than one-half of their former hourly pay rates. Untold thousands of desperate people wandered around the country looking for anything that would give them food for a day and shelter for a night.

The richest, most resourceful country in the world was starting to come apart at the seams like a great ship in a storm when its rudder is disabled.

It was a Presidential election year and the Republicans had been in power for twelve years—all through the Roaring Twenties. Now they pleaded with the electorate for another four years. It would give them time to put the country back on its feet. They still promised: "Prosperity is Just Around the Corner." The "little people" who had borne the brunt of suffering were looking for someone with a new set of slogans.

CHAPTER 3

THE NEW DEAL

F RANKLIN DELANO ROOSEVELT, running as the
Democratic candidate, campaigned on his New Deal
platform dedicated almost totally to a program of financial,
social, and business reform. The Federal Government would
become a real and active instrument to help the people help
themselves. Checks and balances would be set up to guard
against the excesses of the rich and their exploitation of the
poor. Stock markets would be regulated against unscrupulous
manipulators. Banks, savings and savings and loan accounts
were to be insured. The U. S. Government would intercede
against mortgage foreclosures and move vigorously in any
other direction necessary to bring recovery to a dying economy. This included providing jobs for the unemployed
until the private sector of employment could gain enough
momentum to hire the millions of jobless citizens.

The die-hards of the Old Guard called this "Socialism,"
"wildeyed dreams," "irresponsible political promises."
A long suffering population of the "little people" thought
differently and Roosevelt was elected.

The four months interval between Franklin Delano
Roosevelt's election and his inauguration on March 4,
1933 was just as bad, if not worse insofar as the effects of
the depression were concerned. There was, however, a
different feeling—an atmosphere of prayerful hope that the
people would soon have aid and direction to start fighting
their way back to decent conditions.

The world watched and listened to the inaugural speech that spelled out the vast programs that were to be initiated by the new Administration.

The plans were so complex, far reaching, and so revolutionary in scope that the critics said it was impossible, impractical and socialistic. The vast majority, however, said that it was good and that it would work because so many Americans wanted it to succeed and would help to see that it did.

The first priority was to attempt stabilization of the faltering financial situation that by March of 1933 had reached a perilous stage. A bank holiday was called and all banks were closed until proposals for more stability could be explained and implemented. The bank crisis was successfully abated and people breathed easier for the first time in years. This led to the establishment of Federal Deposit Insurance somewhat later.

All State, County, and Municipal taxing agencies were requested to declare a moratorium on penalties for delinquent taxes. Banks and Loan companies were urged to hold back on foreclosures. By summer of 1933 a dozen or more Federal Agencies had been put into being to start the Country on its long, hard road to recovery.

Another Catastrophe

Two weeks after President Roosevelt was inaugurated South Bend experienced a shock greater than any that had occurred during the most hopeless days of the depression. Studebaker Corporation was declared bankrupt and placed under receivership. To the public it was as though the Rock of Gibraltar had sunk into the sea. For Studebaker employees it seemed like the San Francisco earthquake and the Johnstown Flood all in one.

The Company had been the main industry in the community for more than 80 years. Its payroll was the major source of the economic life blood of the whole area. As many as three generations of citizens earned their living there.

With the mood of the depression still predominating, it seemed to the community that Fate had dealt it a monstrously foul blow. Other areas could now see hope in the future but a black cloud of gloom descended over most of the people in South Bend.

Between 1915 and 1930 a hundred or more auto companies had travelled the bankruptcy route. This, the pessimists said, was proof enough that Studebaker was gone forever.

The optimism of the era of recovery, however, took over and under a receivership set up by a Federal Court the plant continued to run.

Despite the stigma of bankruptcy and the obvious financial handicap, the Company's sales held up fairly well for that poverty stricken period. This provided only about two days work per week through April and May but by the end of June, 3 and 4 day weeks had been reached.

F D R Advises Labor

President Roosevelt's most controversial and far reaching innovation came as advice. He said: "If I worked in a factory or a mill the first thing I would do would be to join a union."

Big Business was infuriated almost beyond description. They roared their defiance and vowed to never comply to any demands from their employees. The President was a Socialist, a madman, he would ruin private enterprise, and so on. This tirade gathered momentum of titanic proportions and went on for years.

South Bend had never been noted for union activity. A few building trades unions with not very many members, made up the bulk of the City's then existing unions. There was a smattering of others—possibly a couple of hundred members—with most of those affiliated with Chicago area locals.

Many union organizational attempts had been made in the various South Bend shops as early as 1920 and several more were made during the 20's. Most of these efforts in Studebaker were directed towards single craft groups like trimmers, iron moulders, forge operators, and similar groups. All came to the same sad end after a few months.

Around 1924 several under-cover representatives of IWW became active trying to organize both at Studebaker and among the employees of a few building contractors. A few building trades people joined but they made no progress at Studebaker.

In the late 20's a group of Bendix employees made some vigorous attempts to organize but eventually were defeated and most of them were either fired or quit.

Workers at both Bendix and Studebaker began talking union even before the inauguration of President Roosevelt but work was so slack they seldom could get together long enough to do any planning. By June work had picked up enough to allow the planning to proceed.

By July, 1933, the machinery of recovery proposed by President Roosevelt was beginning to slowly take shape. Federal agencies were set up by Presidential decree and Congressional Legislation to administer the vast complex of national rehabilitation measures needed to refloat the foundered Ship of State.

The Public Works Administration had started to give employment to many of the unemployed adults while the Civilian Conservations Corps (CCC) began to provide jobs for thousands of youths who had never had a job or earned a dollar in their lives. The Home Owners Loan Corporation (HOLC) was saving hundreds of thousands of homes from foreclosure. Federal Deposit Insurance made it safe for people to bring their hoarded money out of hiding and put it into circulation again.

NIRA (National Industrial Recovery Administration) was helping put some semblance of order into the employment practices of the shattered and tangled industries around the country.

These and many other programs were either in operation or on the "drawing boards" to help prime the bone dry pumps of the national economy but even so the critics carped that it would never work.

The Conception of UAW

Late in June a small group of employees from the Studebaker body shops on Lafayette Street began talking seriously about forming a Union. Most of them were body metal finishers from the two northern-most buildings in the huge, sprawling complex of the big multi-stories facilities that made up the several Studebaker plants.

The meetings were held during lunch hour on the Southwest corner of Main and South Streets, about 2 blocks from the plants. By mid-July these gatherings were held almost daily and the interest increased every day. None of the men knew much about Unions but it was the consensus that the American Federation of Labor was the only logical group to join.

A former fellow worker who had been gone for a couple of years stopped by several times and listened to the plans. He projected himself into the discussions and told about having attended a "wonderful school for workers" suggesting that he could give much help toward starting a new and better kind of Union. The AFL, he said, couldn't be trusted because he had learned on good authority that its President, Bill Green, was just then in the process of selling out to the Communists. The group didn't have any faith in his claims but he was asked for more details on the "school" and how he could have information that nobody else had heard of. He was so evasive that everyone felt his motives must be ulterior. Years later it was learned that he was organizing for the "Communist Party Opposition" (CPO) or "Trotzkyites." Their dogma was that the Communist Party was too meek and too conservative!

In the second week of July a small group was picked to contact the AFL for information and advice. They made their initial contact on the 10th and arranged a meeting for the entire group on the 17th.

The first meeting was in the AFL Labor Temple at Lasalle and Michigan. The organizer was Thomas Conboy. The Initiation Fee was $2.00 and the monthly dues $1.00. Seventeen Studebaker employees either had, or borrowed, the $3.00 and they applied for their Federal Labor Union Charter.

On July 19, the organizer met with the contact committee and arranged a meeting to give the obligation of membership to charter members and to present the charter.

On July 21, the meeting was held and Federal Labor Union (FLU) No. 18310 was launched for its maiden voyage.

Ten days later the same ceremony was held for the charter members of Bendix and FLU 18347 was put into commission.

CHARTER MEMBERS OF FLU 18310

Pole Romanowski	Alton Green**
C. L. Alexander	Ray L. Price
Felix Drzazgowski	Glen Arter
W. Viduka*	John Bartee
Daniel Boocher	C. Bernhardt
C. W. Ellsworth	Frank Setty
George Brown	Frank Martinczak
Ben Zioromski	F. Banaszak
David J. Hill†	J. Balaban

*W. Viduka was the number one man to join the union.
**Alton Green was the second man to join.
†The author, James D. Hill.

CHARTER MEMBERS OF FLU 18347

Gerald Cress	Joe B. Morris
Alfred Gwynne	M. R. Nicodemus
H. A. Black	Gustave H. Oland
E. E. Hite	M. E. Tucker
Matt Lee	H. J. Rodgers
Clyde Maples	William J. Gibbons
Felix Goron	L. E. Hoffman
W. Graham	L. E. Moon
John H. Gore	J. R. Poland

CHAPTER 4

ORGANIZING PROBLEMS

AFTER THE embryo Auto Workers at Studebaker had proudly examined their new charter they, for the first time, began to realize the size of the job facing them.

Huge buildings, most of which were multi-storied, spread over an irregular area some three fourths of a mile wide by three miles long. One body shop was 1100 feet by 150 feet with 4 floors plus a basement; the other was 830 feet by 100 feet with 6 floors and a basement. Other buildings were even larger and the parts department, a one story building of some 10 or 12 acres of floor space, was 2 miles removed from the main plant.

The 5500 to 6000 employees they hoped to organize weren't going to be easy to contact. An old company rule, now suddenly dusted off, forbade entry into another department without a pass and notification of the foreman in the department. All but two of the charter applicants worked at the extreme north end of the complex and all of them were now under the constant scrutiny of their supervisors.

Fame Spreads

By mid-autumn of 1933 the activities of the South Bend industrial union pioneers had attracted the attention of people all over the country. It was viewed with alarm by employers as a "threat to America," the "first wedge of Socialism," a "millstone around the neck of Industry" and other titles of dire foreboding. Workers all over the country and in Canada acclaimed it as a giant step towards freedom from exploitation of the masses and promised to join their strength to the movement.

As front runners often do Locals 18310 and 18347 found themselves in demand as advisors and leaders. Long before their own plants were organizationally secure they were spearheading union drives in many South Bend and Mishawaka industries and with remarkable success.

From local activity to a much broader area was the next natural step. Southern Michigan, Elkhart, Laporte and Plymouth workers began to ask for help from the South Benders. The willing and the active of 18310 and 18347 often worked double shifts, one shift in the plant, another in the organizational effort.

Initiation by Installment

The initiation fee was a serious deterrent for many who were otherwise willing. Long accumulated family needs, pressing debts, plus years of low wage rates and short hours had made $2.00 look like a huge sum.

Local 18310 petitioned AFL to waive its payment or at least reduce it but they were turned down. In a desperate attempt to keep organization moving it was decided to spread the $2.00 over an 8 week period at 25 cents per week.

New members came in so fast that all of the union's officers plus others who volunteered were pressed into service at the dues tables. After the office was closed they had to work into the small hours to keep their records posted.

After a couple of weeks the local union was forced to put its Financial Secretary on a full time basis and even then it required many volunteers working late in the night to help him. The installment plan soon ran into trouble on the collecting of the 25 cents per week and this problem went on for many months.

Working Under Receivership

Operating under receivership caused many problems for both management and labor. The Federal Court kept the operation under close scrutiny for many months to see to it that the terms of receivership were strictly met.

More than 100 auto companies had passed out via the bankruptcy route over the years with Studebaker being the first to attempt a recovery. The Judge had been criticized for his decision to allow the plant to continue and he intended to see that his leniency was not abused.

The plant operated on a "month basis"; that is each month's sales were checked and all material purchases had to be paid for that month. Just enough money was released to run the next month. At the end of each month the lines were "run dry," i.e., cleaned off from end to end. Then an inventory was taken of materials used and the other costs involved. Some monthly "runs" lasted for 3 weeks, some a bit more but seldom yielded a full month's work.

Organizing problems at Studebaker were compounded because the "line draining" resulted in the employees at the starting point having to start about a week before the cars reached the final line. Some departments would be home while waiting for the units to reach their stations — when they went to work still others would be off. There was seldom more than 2 weeks out of a month that the entire plant operated with all employees on the job.

By setting up committees in each department to carry on the contacts and by holding almost nightly meetings to coordinate their efforts the recruiters managed to make good progress.

The every month inventory went on into mid autumn until the Federal Court was satisfied that the Studebaker Corporation would survive its bankruptcy.

Knights and Ladies of Mercy

The earliest forerunners of the UAW "standing committees" came about within the first couple of months of the careers of 18310 and 18347. The Sick and Welfare Committees started out as ad hoc departmental groups appointed, or volunteering to raise cash, food, clothing and other assistance for the ill and the destitute.

This practice while helpful to many often missed the most needy cases.

Now with union organizations that covered the entire plants it was learned that the need for assistance was far greater than anyone had ever before realized.

Plant wide committees of both locals went to work on their missions of mercy with such efficiency, dedicated zeal and amazing ingenuity that even the unions' worst detractors applauded. At first the work load of long standing cases seemed hopelessly beyond their capabilities but long hours and willing workers soon had the situation in hand.

Among the legions of unsung heroes of the labor movement's formative days Sick and Welfare Committeemen stand tall and proud.

It became evident very early in the organizational stages that many types of difficulties must be met and overcome. it was equally evident that the AFL was neither willing or able to give any assistance with the more complicated problems.

In fact one of the major obstacles to be overcome was an AFL policy that hadn't even been mentioned during the first phases of organization. After about the 2nd month several of the "old line" craft unions inadvertently revealed that when the plants were finally organized they intended to move in and take over the workers that fitted into their respective Internationals. This included such crafts as machinists, electricians, millwrights, carpenters, laborers, moulders, coremakers and, many others. The Studebaker employees for instance, would have been divided among some 15 or 20 different AFL craft unions. Those that didn't fit into any of the old-line union categories could stay in Local 18310.

The members of both 18310 and 18347 took swift and emphatic action to inform the AFL hierarchy that their greedy intentions would never come to pass. "This is crude and outright cannibalism." they said.

It was the new unions' first good look at the avaricious and mercenary nature of those who then held top offices in too many of the craft unions.

The old-liners pulled back when they saw the hard and firm attitude of their intended victims but their officials let it be known they would be heard from another day. Not all AFL leaders felt the way of the hungry majority and several vigorously supported the position taken by the fledgling groups. Their experience, and their moral support

22

helped the beginners over many rough spots during those first 2 or 3 trying months.

During the hassle many of the practices and shortcomings of the several AFL Internationals came to light. Apprenticeships were restricted to relatives of bosses and business agents and held to such low quotas that far too few craftsmen were trained. Initiation fees were often set far beyond the ability of an average worker to pay. In some cases the initiation fee system was turned into a racket where the new employee would be fired by an accommodating boss as soon as it was paid and thus make room for another candidate who in turn suffered the same fate.

Controlled elections and outright appointments too often assured the perpetuation in office of whoever the heads of a certain few Internationals wanted.

First, second and third class membership status was practiced by several unions. This caste system often forbade any but the "top graders" from participating in their decision making sessions.

These discoveries plus the general attitude of a majority of the craft union leaders convinced the members of 18310 and 18347 that they absolutely must have their own International. Such a union would be run by the democratic process and must work not only for its own members, but for the general welfare of the public. When the locals were still only 3 or 4 months old their determination had been so firmly established that it was only a question of when, not if, an auto International would be formed.

CHAPTER 5

EMBRYO
COLLECTIVE BARGAINING

AFTER SEVERAL MONTHS largely devoted to organizational activity by local 18310 problems began to develop in dues collection. There were numerous reasons but the most voiced ones were that there had been no meeting with corporation officials and no pay increases. The complaints while initiated by anti-unionists soon gained their own momentum and drop-outs increased alarmingly.

After the grace period of non-payment of dues was past the local was forced to suspend the delinquent ones. There were times when suspensions exceeded new applications by substantial percentages.

Local union officials had been waiting for Corporation profits to reach a healthier position but now decided it was too risky to wait any longer. A committee was chosen, management contacted, and the first meeting was arranged early in 1934.

With much trepidation on both sides Studebaker held its first collective bargaining session. After introductions and a few minutes of awkward searching for polite postures the parties were talking on free and friendly terms.

The union spokesmen made no pretense about their critical problems nor about their expectations of a wage increase. Management could not have been unaware of the barely 50 percent paid up membership but were tactful enough to refrain from pushing the point beyond questioning if there was a majority.

Besides wages the union needs included a long list of minor and major items that were submitted for adjustments.

All items were discussed and listed for investigation; a few were settled "on the spot."

The Corporation gave the union committee its first direct and official report on the status of finances including income and expense and explained future hopes and plans. Receivership rules prevented any immediate commitments but they indicated a sympathetic reaction to the union's proposals.

The committee's request for official and written recognition of 18310 as the legal collective bargaining agent was parried but an unspoken consent was clearly implied.

When the results were reported to an eager and curious membership at the next meeting it received warm acclaim, and confidence in their union returned, bigger than ever.

The Long Hard Pull Begins

In their respective shops the novice unionites of both locals soon started to learn the hard lessons of organizing. Very few of the workers knew anything at all about unions but that didn't prevent the opposition side from expounding against it with vigor and volume.

The very idea of a union was an anathema to the Red Apple Corps at Studebaker who had basked in the bosses's favor so long and so lucratively. Their anti-union campaign propaganda was amateurish and full of fiction and fantasy but certainly wasn't lacking in fervor. However, too many people had been waiting too long for an opportunity to get at those bosses' pets and now they meant to enjoy it.

Some 7 weeks after being chartered the adherents of 18347 were confronted with a full fledged company union, the Bendix Employees Association, hereafter called BEA. Their program was: no dues; the bosses like us; no strikes; be loyal to our benefactor, etc., after the pattern of all straw man "unions."

The unionists at Bendix made much faster progress in their organizing drive than was the case at Studebaker. By mid-October they had signed up 1136 members out of the 1446 man work force.

The competition of BEA and the overt and active hostility of the Company seemed to be just the kind of challenges the members of 18347 liked to meet. The smaller and much more compact plant was probably a most helpful factor due to much faster communications and better acquaintance between the employees.

Organizing the workers at Studebaker presented so many frustrating problems that it was determined very early in the effort to follow a military like campaign. Strategy had to be developed to fit each situation and if it didn't work new plans were painstakingly designed to correct the miscalculations. The "Items" below show just a few of the problems.

Item: The plant was so huge and spread out that not one of the first cadre of organizers was familiar with the greater part of it. The only solution appeared to be the concentration of all efforts in the body shops until enough dedicated recruits came in to attack the more distant, unfamiliar, areas. Fortunately the operations in the two body plants were consolidated into the more modern six story building within 5 or 6 weeks after the Union started.

Item: In several whole departments and, some sections of otherwise favorable departments, the supervisors and their stooges had started a hard line of opposition. All visitors were kept under close surveillance and their every move was recorded. Pro union workers were harrassed by the "antis" and the supervisors alike. It was almost impossible to tell friend from foe when making the first contacts.

Item: The world advertised Studebaker practice of hiring whole families, which often resulted in several generations on the Company payroll caused many problems. With a father or grandfather as a foreman, a daughter or sister as secretary to a high official and several other relatives scattered over the plant, the bosses had an efficient made to order spy system in most areas.

Once the decision to cover the body shop first was implemented the campaign moved fast but not without much sound and fury. This area had far more than its share of petty racketeers, bosses pets, and willing company spys all determined not to give up their favored positions of special privileges. But it also had 15 of the 17 charter members who were equally determined to end the reign of coercion, favoritism and tyranny.

On familiar ground and pitted against opponents whose sins and bad habits they knew inside out the 18310 recruiters went to work with enthusiasm. Goaded with fear of losing their "inside track" on favors and infuriated by the exposure of their past misdeeds the Red Apple Corps fought back viciously. Reports of union corruption, whispering campaigns of character assassination, scare stories about plant closings and other rumors of dire forebodings were fabricated and disseminated almost hourly.

Due to the plant being shut down through much of August it was around the second week of September when the drive in the body plant got started. By the first of October some 70% of the 1600 workers in that division had joined plus probably 600 from other parts of the plant. Many new and vigorous organizers had been gained along with a lot of much needed experience on how to, and how not to, go about winning supporters.

All during the period since being chartered, weekly and often semi-weekly meetings were held to report on activities and to assess and reappraise strategy. After about 10 weeks one of the most active union workers summed up the feelings of most of the men. "In the last 2 months I've attended more meetings, learned more, made more mistakes, did more things right and experienced more satisfaction than in all of my past life."

Signs of Maturity

With several hundred new adherents of 18310 in other divisions of the plant, the organization had grown so big that a more comprehensive and sophisticated administration became imperative.

Several temporary committees were formed to promote organization, handle the increasingly abundant membership complaints and to collect dues. Opposition from the anti-union forces was just as bitter as in the body shop but they were now dealing with a group that had the benefit of some 2 or 3 months battle experience. By December the union had established beachheads in every division excepting the foundry and final line and the membership had passed the 3000 mark.

During the July 1933 to January 1934 period Local 18310 had changed several officers due to resignations and was beginning to experience some intra-union friction. Clash of personalities and differences over methods caused so much dissension that progress was hurt.

A considerable number of the newer members had little patience with the "department hopping" technique of organizing. They wanted to shut the plant down to force everyone in and also advocated demanding a big wage increase at the same time.

The cooler heads counselled against any force just then because they feared losing the responsible image that had been established by their carefully considered strategy. They also warned not to strike the company while it was still in so precarious a financial strait. Such rash action couldn't possibly gain anything but the disfavor of the workers and public alike. After a majority were in the union and the company showed a good profit such action might be feasible.

Both the Bendix and the Studebaker Locals had been regularly attending the meetings of the Central Labor Union (CLU), a council of all AFL Internationals in the area, from their beginnings. They requested the Council to put more help into the organizing struggles of the embattled workers in several shops. When they didn't act the officers of various Internationals and Locals were petitioned but the results were meager at the best. Two or three of the officers in old line Locals did however perform dedicated and effective service on the behalf of the unorganized. These few stalwarts and the already over-loaded leaders of the two new Locals took on the job. They made up the sum total of the indefatigable team that helped the workers make South Bend the early capitol of industrial unionism.

A near majority status was attained by 18310 shortly after February 1, 1934, the beginning of its second 6 months. The leaders no longer thought of themselves as novices — they were veterans now — and were beginning to help the workers in other plants.

Oliver, the plow manufacturer was almost as old as Studebaker with some 2000 employees and about the same kind of background. Singer, the maker of sewing machines was comparable to Oliver in size and it too had been in existence for many generations. Both groups of workers were having a rough way to go in their attempts to organize and needed far more help than the new locals could give but AFL either could not, or would not, go to their assistance.

CHAPTER 6

ADVERSARY FROM WITHIN

BEA MADE its debut on September 19 and the next day Local 18347 sent its first request in for a bargaining conference with the Company. The reaction of the vast majority of Bendix employees against the puppet "union" was scorn, outrage, and a burning thirst for action. It was an arrogant insult to their intelligence and they wanted their employer to know just how violently they opposed this cheap subterfuge.

The Corporation however was determined to force their psuedo bargaining agent down the throats of their employees. Their counter attack against 18347's adherents was to initiate a mass layoff to scare and starve the rebels into submission. Nine days after their disdainful rejection of the Company's "toy" nearly 700 members of the bona fide union were on layoff. The Local however knew its rights and how to get them enforced. The U. S. Department of Labor sent a commissioner to town and the Corporation and Union met for the first time on equal terms.

The management soon began to realize that it had over played its hand was now caught in the trap it had set for the unionists. With the Labor Commissioner on the scene and 18347's plus 75 percent signed up majority of the bargaining unit Bendix decided discretion was the better part of valor.

They extricated themselves from their own tangled web by granting a grudging oral recognition of the union. Armed with this most coveted right the Local negotiated the immediate recall of the 700. If necessary they would share and share alike whatever work was available. 18347 had won its first big battle and welded its members into an organization of valiant fighters for justice.

First 6 Months

In their first 6 months both locals had several officer changes. The lot of a union official in those formative days was not pleasant nor economically remunerating; on the contrary it was frustrating, exasperating and almost thankless. Personality clashes were frequent and bitter due to the tension and almost endless hours. Organizing and handling shop problems left little time for record keeping so it is not possible to give the recognition that is due to all those pioneer warriors who served so nobly and so well in that turbulent period.

Although it took several months to obtain meetings with top management both locals dealt with supervision at the department level within a few weeks after being chartered. The directives built into the National Industrial Recovery Administration (NIRA) opened the way and the local unions followed them with vigor and persistence.

With no negotiated contracts but lots of desire to win justice and equity, partiality and discrimination had begun to give way to fair treatment particularly on the issues that could be handled by the lower echelons of supervision. Layoff and recall by senority replaced the Red Apple systems. 18347 took its first strike vote on 1-9-34 over a union busting tactic involving a layoff in the Tool Division in order to get at some local union officers.

Both parties met with NLRB and resolved the issue. The laid-off workers were returned and union prestige gained another notch. A week or so later the Company and the Union met at the South Bend News Times office where a 5c raise in March and another in June were negotiated. Several other significant gains were granted and the strike issues were satisfactorily settled.

Local 18347's organizing efforts had gained 80 percent of the some 1400 eligibles and 18310 had close to 50 percent of its nearly 6000 potentials. Both locals had unwritten but none the less valid recognition as bargaining agents for their respective units.

By trial and error and a dedicated, unremitting, around the clock campaign the once theoretically impractical, and almost impossible, feat of organizing plants in the auto industry was well started.

Very soon after the Indiana auto workers got under way the same effort started in several other states. Wisconsin, Ohio, and Michigan were among the front runners.

Second 6 Months

The period herein covered starts with February 1934 and runs through July. The industrial union movement in America was spreading from border to border, coast to coast. The Nation's economy was still far from robust but vastly improved over the same period in 1933.

Through their city, state and national organizations the Chamber of Commerce and Manufacturer Associations were mounting a massive war on unions. Newspaper editorials, anti-union comic cartoons, paid ads and slanted news items became more prevalent daily. Some of the national magazines joined the fray as did many radio commentators.

Employers began to revert to the illicit pre-New Deal anti-union techniques. Hired labor spies and professional strike breakers came back into use. The old "black-ball" practice was dusted off and put to work against job seekers who had played even a minor role in a union. These and other brutal tactics of underworld terrorism including the kidnapping and beating of labor leaders after the pattern of the 19th Century again became common practice in some industrial centers.

Organizational drives at the Oliver and Singer plants were running into increasingly more serious opposition that had many of the earmarks of being directed by professional union busters. The workers ran into violent opposition from the first day and it never lessened throughout the struggle. Leaders were laid off, some were fired and others beaten up long before they had a chance to gain a majority membership status for their Unions.

The new auto locals helped all they could but their treasuries were too low to furnish the amount of manpower and capital that was needed. They turned to AFL for aid but their coffers hadn't grown so fat from helping beleagured workers organize their shops.

Other drives were beginning to develop in some smaller plants and in the area of service employees. Employer reaction was equally strong in nearly all these cases and particularly so among those providing various types of services.

Again the new locals beseeched AFL to put enough money and men into the effort to give these smaller groups a chance to succeed. Several of the old line Internationals joined in the effort of persuasion and AFL finally started to dole out some token aid.

Both 18310 and 18347 still had many organizational problems to overcome in their own plants. The company union continued to plague the workers at Bendix with sabotage of union programs and continuous under-cutting of the leadership.

At Studebaker work hours were still short, often no more than 3 days per week. Low wages and an on-going hatchet job from the in-plant opposition kept suspensions at a dangerously high level. Collection of dues became such a major problem that it often seemed as though it would never be solved.

The encouragement by union haters to boycott dues had always been an effective weapon against organized labor. Wild rumors about officers playing fast and loose with union funds; gloomy predictions about the Company's chances of survival; plus the all too real grinding poverty added up to a seemingly insurmountable stone wall of trouble.

In the midst of these soul trying tribulations human endurance often reached its limits. Several leaders of 18310 were forced by sheer physical and nervous exhaustion to temporarily reduce, or entirely give up, their union activities. The president was among the many casualties who had to withdraw their valiant services from the battle. President John Kolecki had been in the front lines from the second month of the local's existence and his resignation in March of 1934 was a severe blow to South Bend's struggling labor movement.

Another battle seasoned front line fighter, Russell J. Merrill, stepped into the vacancy and took on the task of leading the fledgling union in its fight for survival. He was to become one of the most noted of all the UAW frontiersmen who helped blaze the thorny trails through the wilderness of the open shops and union hatred.

Dues were the seemingly endless theme at the weekly membership meetings and finally patience wore too thin for further tolerance. The president was given discretion to work out a remedy and pledged support in its application.

Before any meaningful strategy could be developed it was painfully clear that a reorganization of department and division leadership would be necessary. The first move was to adopt the steward system with a group steward for groups of 30 to 40 workers and all group stewards were to be under the direction of a chief steward in each department. Up to then grievance processing, dues collecting, organizing and communications had been handled by the various individuals, with no specific system, who were always too few and too much overworked. In some areas all of these duties had to be carried on by members of the Executive Board because no one else would serve.

The initial steward force was launched in the same department that provided the original (charter) members. Although the objective was 1 steward to 33 members that first attempt got only 5 for some 400 workers. It was however a start that paid big dividends in settled complaints, better communications and a substantial improvement in the dues collected in that department.

With a wealth of experience on what to do and not to do when recruiting new members, a new and better coordinated organizing committee system was started. After a few weeks of experimentation and indoctrination of a few new recruiters' results in the pilot departments began to prove the worth of the revamped techniques. Despite all of the careful planning, hard work and long hours it was still to be several months before the collection of dues problem could be successfully solved.

The officers and other leaders of 18310 and 18347 ranged farther and farther from home base to help workers in a dozen or so surrounding towns. Shops in Niles, Buchanan, St. Joseph, Benton Harbor, Kalamazoo and several other cities had joined in the drive to be organized. The harvest was indeed great but the workers few!

CHAPTER 7

UNION DEMOCRACY
IS CHARTED

BEFORE THEIR first year ended and despite stubborn opposition from AFL Old Guard leaders the auto unionites made significant headway towards forming their own International. Correspondence by mail and phone and in person with like minded union leaders in Wisconsin, Michigan and Ohio resulted in a plan to form a National Automotive Council. This they hoped would be the vehicle that would eventually carry them to their much coveted International Union of Auto Workers.

In early June of 1934 delegates from the several states met at the Morrison Hotel in Chicago to discuss and plan the hoped for council. Three weeks later the first national conference of their locals was held at the Fort Shelby Hotel in Detroit.

The National Auto Council idea was approved and rules were adopted for its operation. Resolutions calling for immediate and affirmative action towards formation of their own International were adopted and submitted to the AFL. Truly UAW was past the "gleam in the eye" stage!

Forrest G. Woods was elected 18310's National Automotive Council delegate where he served with great distinction.

The conservative wing of the AFL leadership was alarmed at this militant action of the "Young Turks" and reacted by setting up (mostly from their own faction) a Board of Administration to "lead" the upstart insurgents.

After months of unavailing efforts to get some forward motion from the Board of Administration, the Council was forced to work around them. It was all too plain that the

Board had been designed to stifle instead of help the organization of industrial employees. A substantial majority of the new locals were becoming convinced that little progress could be made until they found a way to throw off the smothering influence of the AFL Old Guard.

They turned to the few but militant liberals and progressives among the AFL leaders and found supporters who agreed that the workers in the auto industry needed and must have their own Union.

It was plain even as early as mid-1934 that progress by the American Labor Movement could never be great under the direction of the AFL's ruling dynasty as it was then constituted.

Public Abhorrence Lessens

The attitude of the South Bend business and professional people towards unions at the beginning was varied. It ranged from a very few favorables to the mild disfavor of some to an open raging hostility by the majority. The least prosperous of the city's two daily newspapers was friendly in a neutral sort of way but the prosperous one with a vastly greater circulation faithfully reflected the burning animosity of its big advertisers.

A union wag commented: "Labor in South Bend has a couple of railroad car loads of friends downtown." He squelched his dissenters by adding—"hand car loads— that is."

Those supporters in the public sector consisted of a couple of attorneys, a few doctors, and merchants, a dozen or so school teachers, and a sizable contingent of clergymen.

They were true friends indeed, because their friendly stance for Labor was anything but popular in the business oriented community.

By the end of that first year some amazing improvements in public attitudes had been won. The unions' disciplined behavior, carefully considered demands, concern for the sick, the needy, and the underprivileged, and their unswerving loyalty to the American system all registered favorably. Said the wag: "We can fill a couple of day coaches now!"

Second Year Starts a Lesson in Politics

When the new locals reached their first anniversaries in July, 1934 it seemed to the leaders that it had been ages instead of only a year. One union sage said, "We started with nothing, we still ain't got much, but we've sure carved out one hell of a big hunk of history for the working class."

The yearling locals began to notice more and more that the conservative wing of AFL, both local and national, were definitely beginning to chill towards them. At first this was attributed to their continual pestering of the parent union for the so badly needed additional money and manpower to meet the rapidly developing tide of new potentials. A tip off from the liberal elements of AFL said the real cause of the coolness was political worry that factory union membership would soon outstrip that of the older unions. The Old Guard feared the new crop of militants might some day oust them from their entrenched positions of power!

This explained many things and made it even more important to strive harder to form an Auto Workers International Union. They needed this to consolidate their strength and coordinate the efforts of the automobile and auto parts plants employees who in some 10 or 12 different areas were having a rough way to go in their uphill fights to organize.

At various times during the spring of 1934 delegates from 18310 and 18347 had attended conferences where other auto and auto parts workers were present. All of them had the same desire but Old Guard AFL advice was—"You guys are too pushy for your own good. You have to learn to crawl before you walk." With the exception of the South Benders and one or two others, the new locals had very few members signed up and almost no money in their treasuries. As much as they resented the AFL brush-off they were as yet in no position to rebel.

The progressive liberal wing of the Federation vigorously opposed the attitude of their conservative colleagues and stepped up their own contributions of both money and men.

Graduate Unionists Set Priorities

The South Bend auto locals entered their second year with two top priorities. Number 1 was an International of their own; number 2 was to negotiate formal contracts with their employers. It was becoming increasingly more evident that number 1 might be an even tougher objective to attain than number 2.

Membership dropouts continued to be a critical problem for 18310 while 18347 had to contend with the Company union clamped around its neck like the Old Man of the Sea. What however had seemed so big and unconquerable 6 months earlier now diminished as the unions' experience and expertise increased. The kindergarten unionists of mid-1933 thought of themselves as old pros a year later.

The harsh lessons of the Big Depression were still painfully burned into the minds of the union members. Especially so were the unnecessary privations and hardships caused by the political neglect and indifference of a Big Business oriented Congress. Labor set another priority to fight for the election of good legislators and to oppose the bad ones with every bit of energy they could muster. "Elect our friends, defeat our enemies," an old slogan of organized labor that had fallen into sad disuse during the late '20's was enthusiastically revived. People who had never before put much value on their votes now began to equate them with food on the table and roofs over their heads. That October saw the leaders of 18310 and 18347, already overburdened with their other tasks, take on the job of getting their memberships prepared to vote.

In this new arena the union oriented and sophisticated pros found themselves once again in the role of novices. The old pro politicians of both parties fiercely resented the entry of the potentially powerful newcomers into their private preserves. Liberal Democrats however were so fed up with the ineffective and selfish habits of too many of their own party leaders that they welcomed the unionists and their humane progressive views with open arms. Liberal Republicans around South Bend were practically extinct and the GOP hard-liners added the word "union" along with Roosevelt and the New Deal as new anathemas.

The membership reaction to their leaders' participation in politics was mixed. The majority favored it, many others were doubtful and some of the generations old Republicans were diametrically opposed. However, even the most vociferous of the GOP's champions agreed to take a long hard look before voting for politicians who would wreck the union movement. The effects of the Big Depression still hurt too much to forget or forgive the stupid and heartless ideologies and policies that had brought it about.

The union workers in the off-year election of 1934 performed yeomen service to help elect those who seemed to be friends. They were, however, unhappy about their something less than cordial treatment from party leaders. This feeling grew into a strong conviction that either the politicians must respond to peoples' real needs or a new party should be started. Finding a solution to Labor's political needs became an on-going priority second to none.

Growing Pains

The stresses and strains of a year and a half of all-out effort, of 7 day weeks and 18 hour days began to show.

Tired of continuous bickering, ridiculous rumors and poor cooperation on the part of many members the Officers and Executive Board members of 18347 on February 21, 1935 turned in their individual resignations en masse. "This," they said, "will give our fault finders a chance to do all of the things they have been demanding from us."

The people in attendance at that membership meeting were shocked into a sudden realization of the abuse and shabby treatment being suffered by their leaders. They rejected the resignations and vowed that their obligations to their union would no longer be neglected and that the troublemakers must be dealt with.

The Indispensables

The most exacting, gruelling, and thankless job was that of the Financial (Executive) Secretary. With no previous training, the most primitive of facilities, a seemingly endless chain of complications, plus an overabundance of extra demands, he was indeed an overworked and harried individual.

At 18347 Walter Saxton started from scratch and set up, through the time honored system of trial and error, one of the best offices of that early era. No day was ever too long but for him to take enough time out to help the individuals seeking help or advice "from the Union."

Alton Green at 18310 performed his oft times nightmarish type of job without complaint and always seemed anxious and happy to help the troubled. He was the main liaison agent between the several auto locals throughout the country in their campaign for an International Union. His tireless and dedicated persistence kept the pipelines open through some most trying times.

The South Bend Labor Movement owes much to these two faithful servants.

PHOTO SECTION

The history of the UAW in the South Bend area is here recorded in pictures . . . a little action . . . and many personalities. We offer no apologies for the quality of the pictures . . . they were taken with Brownie Hawkeyes, vest pocket cameras, simple box cameras and what have you? The prints were discovered in bureau drawers, old file cabinets, borrowed from the top of pianos and anywhere we could get them. They weren't gathered for a photo contest . . . they were gathered for you. We hope they bring back memories to our older readers and inform our younger members.

Law by Club and Bomb

SCENE NO. 1: Schultz Trailer Plant, Elkhart, Indiana — Autumn of 1938 — vapor is tear gas. The occasion was when some 30 heavily armed policemen attacked a dozen UAW advocates passing organizational leaflets. Even in those days the incident was noted for its wanton brutality.

SCENE NO. 2: International Representative E. J. "Mose Kucela protects his injured head as O. A. Richardson (with cigar) and two others start him to the hospital. He was struck from behind by a policeman's club as he attempted to reason with the policemen's commanding officer.

More volunteers from Locals 5 and 9 arrived a few minutes later and the odds disappeared as did the riot sticks, guns, and tear gas.

The Schultz employees became the first UAW Local in Elkhart!

ABOVE: WIESS "DICK" VIDUKA was the number one man to pay his $2.00 initiation fee and $1.00 dues to the A F L. On July 10, 1933 as a member of the Studebaker employees contact committee he became the first of untold thousands of South Bend Auto workers. The other 15 charter members joined on July 17. That was the date they received their first pay checks in three weeks!

A B O V E: A L T O N GREEN Local No. 5, was the number two man to pay the $3.00 to A F L towards 18310's charter. An active and efficient organizer from the first day he converted many doubtfuls into an army of positives.

When the dues and initiation fee collection and recording became a titanic task, Alton Green was drafted as Executive (Financial) Secretary. He not only proved to be an expert at that job but also turned out to be an excellent public relations representative and a talented writer for the area and regional Labor papers.

His death in 1950 was mourned by Local No. 5 and all of the Labor people who had known him.

LEFT ABOVE: JOHN BARTEE was one of the seventeen charter members. He had been an active member of the Street Car Union in Indianapolis. He was also a professional wrestler of some renown. There were no members who worked harder or put in longer hours for the Union. From his own funds he purchased much of the educational material of those early times. An indefatigable data and statistics gatherer, his material stood the Unions in good stead on many occasions.

He served the Local as Recording Secretary, Executive Secretary, Vice President and Divisional Representative.

Indiana was the first state to set up a C I O State Council and John was its first Secretary-Treasurer. From that post he played a big role in building C I O into the powerful structure that it finally became.

He then joined the Region 3 staff where his data and statistic collecting added to his other duties made him one of the most oustanding of U A W's loyal adherents.

RIGHT ABOVE: DANIEL BOOCHER was a Charter member of Local 18310. Dan worked hard and effectively in the organizing crusades. He was steward and chief steward for many terms and served as Divisional Representative from 1949 to 1951.

ABOVE: JAMES D. "RED" HILL. Charter (appears as David J. Hill on Charter) member and Organizer in the Body Shop. First Steward in the founding group of Metal Finishers. Chief Steward 5 years, Divisional Representative 6 full and 2 partial terms and President 2 terms, 1949-1951. Served on International Union Staff from May of 1951 until time of Retirement on July 1, 1967.

Started shop paper in 1940 as a mimeographed monthly and developed it into a multilithed weekly called The Studebaker Local No. 5 News.

Helped develop and served on many of the Local's Standing Committees.

ABOVE: ED WINTERS, LOCAL 5, was one of the original organizers in the Studebaker foundry. He served the Union in many roles including Educational Committeeman and steward. As a temporary International organizer in Indianapolis he proved to be a most effective recruiter for U A W.

ABOVE: CHESTER RALSTON was the first Treasurer of Local 18310. He was noted as one of the most forceful and effective of the early leaders.

He also served as Vice President for several partial terms during the organizational period of the Local. President from 1938 until 1941 Chet rendered

invaluable assistance to the International Union while Homer Martins forces sought to wreck it.

He helped form the Studebaker Employees Federal Credit Union and was instrumental in exposing the extortion practices of the loan sharks.

After spending some time as an organizer for U A W Region 3 he became a conciliator for the U. S. Department of Labor in 1942. He served in the capacity until his death on June 11, 1964.

LEFT: HARRY RODGERS was one of the pioneer organizers who helped put the group together that applied for the 18347 charter in July, 1933.

Always an active and militant union member he served the Union in many capacities. He was President from March 1944 to March 1945.

RIGHT: A charter member of Local 18347, **James Poland** was a prime mover in setting up the charter group. He was one of the many Bendix men who helped recruit members in the shops around South Bend.

Because of his organizing ability his Local Union sent him to many other areas where he brought thousands of new people into the Union.

After the formation of C I O and U A W Jim became a recruiter for both groups. Evansville was a large automotive manufacturing town and he was successful in bringing most of the plants into U A W.

He worked on organizational drives in central and western Illinois, northern Kentucky, and over most of Indiana.

Jim was a frontliner in Labor's ranks in its most hectic and critical days.

UAW TRAIL BLAZERS. Carl Shipley, President (right-top) and Virgil F. McGee, Vice president (right-bottom) as they appeared in 1967, some 34 years after they made their first tracks on the long trail to industrial democracy.

These two frontiersmen headed the Local 18347 Committee that won the first agreement from their employer. Others on that historymaking committee were: Walter B. Saxton, Robert Hamilton, Elmer Gollnick, Jack Peterson, M. R. Nicodemus, and William J. Dunn. The agreement reinstated a large number of workers who were laid off in a union-busting attempt; guaranteed day rate pay when 100% efficiency couldn't be attained; payment for waiting time over one hour; a 5% increase on 3-1-34 and another 5% on 6-1-34. For that period in history it was the first big break-through and was hailed as a great triumph by all of Labor.

Shipley served his Local as President until May of 1936, the most significant of UAW's formative years. During his administration Local 18347 sponsored the conference in Chicago on June 3, 1934 where the auto and auto parts workers formally resolved to start their own International Union.

Carl served as Financial Secretary from March, 1938 until March of 1943. He then went to Washington, D.C. to serve as a Labor member of the War Labor Board. After the end of the war he served on the Wage Stabilization Board until 1948 when he went into business for himself.

The Industrial Labor Movement profited much because there was a Carl Shipley.

LEFT: WALTER SAXTON, early in January of 1935 Walter was put on a full time basis as Financial Secretary. As the infant Local was fighting to exist the dues and membership records were the very life line that kept them afloat. In this most critical and sensitive position Walter's dedicated and skillful service was powerful aid to his Local Union's success. He served in the office from 1933 until 1938.

His next union duty was as International Union organizer in the Saginaw, Michigan area. Many new U A W Locals came into being in and around Saginaw because of his four (4) years on the job there.

After his tour of duty as an International Organizer he served his Local as President from 1947 to 1948.

RIGHT: THOMAS JEFFERS was elected President of Local No. 9 on May 17, 1936 and served until January 5, 1939. Under his leadership the Local's organizational efforts continued to spread over an ever increasing radius. On one of their many organizing trips, this one to Three Rivers, Michigan, Jeffers and four (4) other Local 9 organizers were involved in an auto accident. One man, Charles Willard, died and Jeffers was so seriously injured that he was incapacitated for several months.

Tom was one of the leaders in Labor's efforts to start a Farmer Labor Party in Indiana.

In November of 1936 he led his Local Union to a most significant victory in their sitdown strike. It was the first in U A W's precedent setting defeats of Big Industry.

Before becoming President he served the Local as Trustee and as a Bargaining Committeeman.

He passed away on December 29, 1957.

LEFT: CHESTER WILSON of Local 5 was born and bred a union man. Chet always refused union office, but never refused union duty. In the raw, early days when the local operated on a bluff and a prayer—he was the anchor man who rallied the rank and file support to protect their leaders flanks.

RIGHT: ED LEWIS was a steward, chief steward and guide for many terms in Local 5. Ed was a good leader and a loyal and faithful follower. Brother Lewis was always where the need was greatest. His sagacious advice and talented peace-making rendered great service to the local and made him one of its most popular officers.

LEFT: WILLIAM GREGORY, of Local No. 5, was one of the first organizers in the Body Hardware and Trim Department. He was a steward, chief steward, Master Steward, and Vice President. He served one term as President from 1948 to 1949.

RIGHT: JOHN KOLECKI, of Local No. 5, organized the nucleus of Studebaker foundry organizing committee which worked for more than two years to get a majority into the Union.

He was elected President in December of 1933 but had to resign in March 1934 due to illness.

LEFT: ROY GARLIT, of Local 5. Coming from the coal country of Indiana, Roy was a union man by instinct. He served as steward and divisional representative and was a resourceful planner of union strategy. A good diplomat and an astute political observer, he served the union well inside and outside the shop.

RIGHT: O. A. RICHARDSON of Local 5, helped organize the Studebaker Machine Shop and served several terms as Steward.

He was a Divisional Representative, Trustee, Vice President, and President of the CIO Industrial Union Council of St. Joseph County.

ABOVE: EDWARD NICK (Olivers) was member No. 8 on the Charter of Local No. 112 of the Farm Equipment Workers Union. He was an unrelenting frontline fighter against the long and bitter opposition of the Barons of the farm implement industry.

When, after 15 years of uphill struggle, the majority of FE members decided that UAW was their proper base, Eddie helped lead the way. They came into UAW in 1951 as Local No. 1095 and he became No. 8 on that Charter!

Always a dynamic and militant leader he served many terms as a Steward and Bargaining Committeeman.

On the all too numerous picket lines where the odds were bad, the presence of Eddie Nick was a most reassuring factor.

ABOVE: CARRIE Mc-COY was elected President of Oliver's Office Workers Local No. 153, Farm Equipment Workers International Union in 1950. In 1951 she helped lead her membership from FE to UAW where they were chartered as Local No. 1096. Elected as the new U A W Local's first President she has been re-elected each time up to the publishing date of this account 1970.

Among the legions of dedicated unionists in South Bend, Carrie deserves top rating. Her devotion to Labor's cause has been proven many times on picket lines and in organizational drives where it really counted.

ABOVE: VANE L. "SKINNY" BURGOYNE of Local No. 5 helped organize his door aligning group in the department where the charter members originated. He then moved to Body Hardware and Trim and continued his organization activity.

He served as steward, chief steward, Divisional Representative, and Vice President. He was President from 1943 to 1944.

He then went on the staff of Region 3 and became involved in organizational activities in Indiana, Illinois, and Kentucky. He also serviced many Locals and helped them acquire the technique of winning grievances.

RIGHT: ELVIN SMITH, Local 1095, was one of the earliest of Oliver employees to fight for the union cause. A ruthless management aided by professional union busters crushed their first attempts, but two years later (in 1936) a battle wise group triumphed. They became one of the first Locals in the Farm Equipment Workers (FE-CIO).

RIGHT: JOHN SCHAFFER, Local 112 FE, was Local 112's second President and helped lead his embattled Local to victory against heavy odds. The Farm Equipment Industry fought the unions powerfully and bitterly with every dirty trick that the Union-hating professional strike breaker could conceive. Hardened by the starve out - freeze out of that bitter cold winter of 1934-1935 when they lost their first round, the Oliver workers proved tougher than the toughest of the union busters.

E. J. "MOSE" KUCELA was the hard hitting organizer who was largely responsible for organizing the Studebaker Machine Shop that was among the last of the holdouts. He was steward, chief steward, and Divisional Representative and played an important role in the CIO's early days.

He served on the UAW staff for nearly 20 years where he was instrumental in helping organize many shops that had been put on the impossible list. Promoted to assistant Regional Director he held that post until 1961 when ill health forced him to go on disability retirement. He died on February 17, 1968 at age 61.

RUSSELL J. MERRILL, was elected President of U A W Local No. 5 in March of 1934 and served three and one half terms. At U A W;s 1936 convention he was elected to the International Executive Board to direct the Local Unions in Indiana. In 1937 at the Milwaukee convention he was elected one of the first Regional Directors with Indiana as his Region. After leaving the office he was an International Representative until retirement in 1968.

Russ was at the helm of Local 18310 during the hectic and difficult days as it struggled first for survival and then to help build a better world for workers to live in.

On the early day picket lines and organizational campaigns the name Merrill was legion. Neither physical nor verbal assaults ever deterred him in Labor's pitched battles against the union busters and strike breakers.

He led negotiations for Local 5's first contract which was the most comprehensive of that period and a model for years to come.

ABOVE: HARLEY ASHBY of Local No. 5, served six terms as trustee 1938-1944; His good business judgement helped keep the treasury growing; he organized skillfully through the early, rough periods.

ABOVE: T. FORREST HANNA of Local No. 5 served many terms as Steward and as a member of the Local's Standing Committees. He was Recording Secretary, Vice President, and President from 1957 to 1959.

ABOVE: FRANK FISHER of Local No. 5, Chief Organizer in the Body Shop Paint Department. Steward and Chief Steward for many terms, he was the anchor man in his area. His level head and sage advice saved his fellows from many bad situations when the Red Apple Corps still outnumbered the Unionists 10 to 1.

ABOVE: JESS HARRELL o Local No. 5, served 8 years a Recording Secretary and years as Financial Secretary In the hectic days of 1933 and 1934 he was a resourcefu organizer and capable leader

RAYMOND H. BERNDT

He became Secretary of the Local 5 negotiating committee in 1937, elected Recording Secretary in 1938, Financial Secretary in 1941 and 1942, Vice President (Automotive Division) in 1943, and President in 1944 and 1945.

He was one of UAW's chief strategists in CIO's unremitting war on Communism in the 1940's.

Ray worked through the War Labor Board to win millions of dollars for local 5 despite the war-time wage freeze.

After the war he directed the negotiations and won for the Local its Health and Welfare Plan. It was the first among the C I O Unions which had been tailored to the Local's specific planning and it also was administered by the Local.

Elected Regional Director of Region 3 in November of 1947. At the time of this writing he is serving his twenty-third (23rd) year as Director.

His efforts in that capacity have brought scores of new locals and many thousands of new members into UAW.

The fires of adversity and the flames of conflict tempered him well for his role of top flight Union Leader.

His record will hang high in Labor's Hall of Fame.

ABOVE: HAZEL LUCZYK, among the earliest of female organizers at Studebaker, Hazel's dedicated efforts came when most needed. Served several terms as Steward and was a leader in the crusade for equal rights for women.

ABOVE: JANE HUDZINSKI of Local No. 5. Among the early in-plant organizers, there was none more dedicated or active than Jane. From the start of the original drive until 100% membership was attained, she gave the Union her best efforts.

She served the Union in many capacities and contributed much to its success.

ABOVE: LOUIS J. HOR-VATH, served Local 5 as Steward, Chief Steward, Divisional Representative, and Vice President.

He was President from 1952 until 1955. He died in May of 1957.

ABOVE: WILLIAM OGDEN
of Local 5. As an early member of the first plant wide organizing committee (1934) he helped organize the Spring Shop, Stamping Division, and other areas in his vicinity.

Served as a Divisional Representative and helped negotiate Local 5's first contract. Was Vice President four terms - 1938-1941 and from 1964 to 1965. Elected President for four terms - 1941, 1942, 1951, and 1955.

ABOVE: JULIA HORVATH
of Local 5. She was one of the most effective of the early organizers. She led a parade of women to plant No. 8 to show the girls there that they needn't fear to join the union.

ABOVE: GEORGE HUPP,
Local No. 5, Steward and Chief Steward of Motor Assembly Department. Divisional Representative and Vice President of the Aviation Division 1945 to 1946. President in 1946 and 1947.

He was elected State Representative to the Indiana Legislature in 1942.

Bill's youth was spent in the coal mines of Indiana where the Miners Union had fought so long and so valiantly against employer exploitations. His Union parentage and his early battles fitted him well for his leadership roles that were so badly needed in UAW's infancy.

FRANKFURT/GERMANY, DEC. 20, 1949: Gifts for German children from the people of South Bend, Indiana arrived at Rhein-Main Airport to-day aboard an American Overseas Airlines Stratocruiser. The three hundred pounds of clothing and candy were donated by the Bendix Local No. 9 Union, South Bend, in response to an appeal by 1st Lt. John S. Pallatin, a former Union member and now Special Service Officer in the 4th Constabulary Squadron in Hersfeld, Germany. The request for Christmas presents were made through the radio and newspapers and an additional one thousand pounds of gifts were sent.

Photo shows: Lt. Pallatin helps unload the gifts from the airplane as two of his GYA children look on.

CIVIL DEFENSE

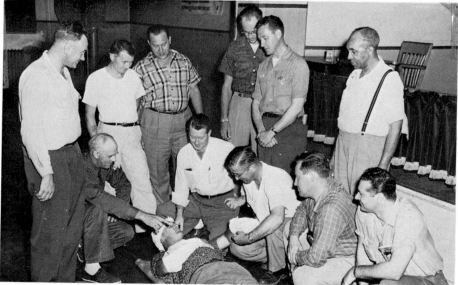

LOCAL 5's CD unit demonstrates emergency techniques.

Seated left to right: A Red Cross instructor, Bob Hagenbush, Mike Lenyo, Joey Andrews and John Balatore.

Standing left to right: Ken Anderson, James Flora, J. D. Hill Jr., Neil Moorlag, Glen Andrews and Ed Lewis. ("Patient" unidentified.)

SOUTH BEND: Local 9's award winning float in 1956 when UAW celebrated the 20th anniversary of its first free convention held in South Bend in 1936.

SOUTH BEND: PRESIDENT REPORTS. "Big" Nick reports to the membership on the happenings at the convention. Members of the Executive Board sit back of him.

TEETERBORO, N. J.: BENDIX COUNCIL MEETS. Standing, left to right: Al Rall, Teeterboro, Bob Bridges, South Bend; Mike Hart, Norwood, Mass.; Ed Wygant, South Bend; Ralph Hershberger, South Bend; Vendetta Nick, South Bend. Seated, left to right: Stanley Cooke, Hollywood, Calif.; Don Zolman, South Bend; Phil Carpenter, South Bend; James Carroll, Detroit and Fritz Quatrini, Elmira, N. Y.

SOUTH BEND: ON THE BRICKS: "Big" Nick carries the picket banner in Local 9's 74-day strike in 1949. In the first week of the strike Local 5's 21,000 members voted to assess themselves $1.00 per week for the duration to support their neighbor unionists. Other Unions around the Country also rallied to their support.

SOUTH BEND: SUMMIT NEGOTIATIONS:UAW President Walter P. Reuther and Regional Director Raymond H. Berndt help Local 9's Bargaining Committee settle their 1949 strike in Washington, D.C. The Union won all points at issue.

SITDOWN! SITDOWN!

SOUTH BEND: SIT DOWN! LOCAL NO. 9 sit down strikers gather round their music makers as they all hold the fort. They stayed in six days and won all points at issue. It was the first sit down strike in the history of American labor unions.

SOUTH BEND: FEMININE SIT-DOWNERS OF LOCAL 9. Scene is in basement of Plant 3. It happened in November of 1936.

WAKEMAN HOSPITAL AT CAMP ATTERBURY GETS PIONEER COMMUNITY SERVICE FROM LOCAL 5

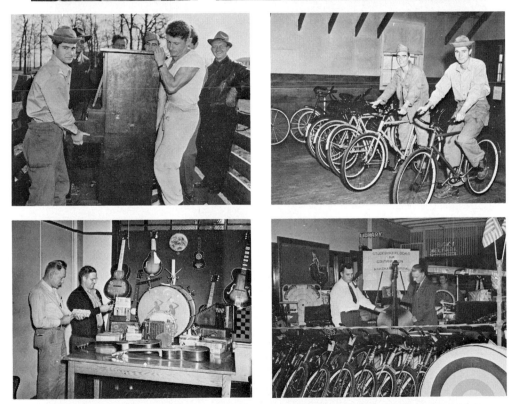

Local 5, in 1943 and 1944, contributed truckloads of supplies to Wakeman Veterans Hospital at Camp Atterbury. Photo top left shows J. D. Hill accepting a saxaphone from donor. Top right photo shows Red Hill and Ray Berndt of Local 5 inspecting machine tools a large mercantile establishment contributed to the drive. Center left a happy G.I. helps unload a piano and center right the first shipment of bikes arrive. Bottom right shows John Szabo Jr. and Local 5 President Ray Berndt inspecting a large shipment of supplies and bottom left photo catches J. D. Hill and Frank Odell, committee members contemplating their collection of contributed musical instruments.

CONVENTION

ATLANTIC CITY: 1946 U A W CONVENTION: James McEwan, Charles Clemans, Vendetta Nick, and Herschel Davis discuss strategy. Walter P. Reuther was elected at this convention.

ATLANTIC CITY: CAUCUS: It is said that whenever two or more Auto Workers meet there is a caucus. Here "Chuck" Clemans "Big" Nick and Jim McEwan caucus on Reuther's chance of unseating R. J. Thomas at the 1946 convention in Atlantic City.

WE CARED!

Local No. 5's Recreation Committee presents the St. Joseph County Orphanage with gymnasium equipment. It included a boxing ring, punching bags, gloves, bar bells, ping pong tables, a shuffleboard set, and other items too numerous to mention.

Seated: A sporting goods salesman; man in topcoat is an agent from the Children's Home. Others, left to right: Paul Daniels, Ralph Boles, Napoleon Callewart, Louie Robb, Gene Little, Ted Vanscoyk, Maurice Cohen, and J. D. Hill, President of the Local.

SOUTH BEND: Local No. 9's Welfare Committee prepares Christmas baskets for the sick and needy. Standing, left to right: Lillian Quimby, (second lady unknown), Carl Shipley, Bob Houston, Mrs. James McEwan and Henry Wheeler.

In front are Peter Ruppert, Committee Chairman and President Thomas Jeffers.

SANTA'S HELPERS

LOCAL NO. 5 RECREATION COMMITTEE and helpers pack Christmas boxes for children in West Germany in November 1946. #1 is Walter Hill, #2 Clarence Hoctel and #3 is Napoleon Callewart.

. . . and that's our pictures of the early days of the union and UAW in the area where UAW was born in Region 3 . . . they aren't good in many cases . . . but they aren't too bad in some instances either. They all tell a story of dedication and sacrifice in the struggle to make a better world.

We used photos from contemporary sources, wherever possible, although later and better pictures may have been available.

We appreciate the cooperation of many persons in lending the pictures to us. We thank them sincerely.

CHAPTER 8

THE TEMPLE
OF INDUSTRIAL LABOR

T HE NEW LOCALS soon outgrew their downtown quarters in the 300 block of South Michigan Street and looked for a more spacious home. 18310 rented a large three story building at 919 South Michigan Street and 18347 also moved there. For years to come this was to be the Capitol Building of industrial unionism in the midwest.

Here came the delegates bent on having their own Internationals and many a hard-up delegate slept there to save on his meager expense allowance.

Small unions with little money found in it a haven for meetings and a place to use as an address. Around its spacious halls and offices there was a glowing aura of brotherhood and compassion totally lacking in the stuffy atmosphere of the old AFL headquarters.

Broken Promises

Long before the end of 1934 it became apparent that AFL promises to launch a massive organizing drive were in trouble. Despite the fact that most of the crafts seemed to genuinely want to do it, the controlling majority of the Executive Council still refused to budge. Insiders reported that about a half dozen of the more powerful among the Old Guard remained adamant in their intentions to dismember the factory locals for their own assimilation.

In some places angry members started dropping out by the thousands. It was estimated that in the Detroit-Flint area as many as 75 percent of the auto workers in FLU locals rejected AFL. Some started independent unions while others waited for AFL reform. The South Benders decided to stay with it and try to reform from within.

Viewed in retrospect, 1934 was a good year for progress by the South Bend Unionists. In the heat of the battle, however, it didn't seem so great.

Gaining a Little Momentum

The first Constitution and By Laws were adopted by both locals during 1934. Article II, Aims and Objects, from 18310's document expressed the ideals and objectives of the budding movement.

> To unite in one organization, regardless of creed, color, sex or nationality, all workmen eligible for membership employed in the manufacturing of automobiles within the Studebaker factory or factories, except company representatives, such as foremen, assistant foremen and anyone having authority over the employees.
>
> To adopt, carry out, and put into operation an effective plan for keeping its members employed.
>
> To provide means for the intellectual development of its members and to educate them in the principles of unionism.
>
> To stimulate the political education of the members to understand their political rights and to use the ballot intelligently and induce others to do likewise, to the end that the Government may be a government for, of and by the people and not be used as a tool to further the ends of combinations of employers.

Toward the end of 1934 Studebaker was showing a small but steady profit so the subject of a pay raise was revived. Although only a 5 cents across the board was gained it brought great rejoicing. It was the first plant-wide raise gained by any of the basic automobile manufacturing unions. (Bendix was involved in parts for both automotive and aircraft.)

From all sections of the sprawling Studebaker complex a spontaneous chorus was raised for the delinquents and holdouts to get into the union or out of the shop. Even before the demand reached full voice the President of 18310 called his staff together and proposed a bold go-for-broke effort. The word went out that on a given date the union members would no longer work with non-members. With the outcry of "pay up you slackers" coming from all points the hitchhikers got on the ball! The downtown union office had lines reminiscent of the depression dole lines. From time to time after that holdouts and delinquents caused some vexing problems but the big worry was over!

Professional Union Busters

By the last half of 1934 union organizing efforts had vastly increased but so had employer resistance. Many companies had reverted to the infamous union smashing tactics of the past but there was now a new spirit of worker independence. This plus a true friend in the White House gave the union minded both the courage and the inspiration to take on their well heeled opponents.

The repertoire of stratagems used by the professional union busters was almost limitless. Night riding thugs, character assassins, inplant spies, rumor fabricators, experts at forming company unions and so on ad infinitum were on their illicit lists. Disbarred lawyers, ex-bootleggers, ex-convicts and shady denizens of the underworld found it a lucrative field.

Under cover of darkness, fictitious names and titles, and frequent changes of characters it was almost impossible to identify the guilty ones. It was something often felt but seldom seen!

Struggle for organization at Olivers, Singers and several smaller shops reached critical stages in the fall. Although substantial numbers had joined the unions their efforts to build effective organizations were frustrated time after time. There were plenty of symptoms of professional union-breaking but little tangible proof until the workers at Oliver were forced to strike. Even then the only evidence was the sudden disappearance of the "new men" who had been the main strike agitators! Similar strategy at Singers and a couple of smaller plants also resulted in strikes that were disastrous to many of the workers. There too the key agitators had been recent hires who faded away as soon as their manipulated walkouts took place.

The South Bend laborites had learned a new lesson that stood them in good stead many times in the turbulent years to come.

New Players—Old Coaches

By early 1934 the South Bend Locals were establishing a rapport with the more visionary of the old line leaders.

The United Mine Workers, the Amalgamated Clothing Workers, the Typographical Union, the Ladies Garment Workers, the Textile Workers and several smaller Internationals seemed to have the philosophy the new unions sought.

It was an open secret that these liberal unions had long been waiting for an opportunity to challenge the hide-bound policies of the Old Guard controlled AFL Executive Council. The foot-dragging on the organization of industrial plants presented the issue they had waited for.

Under their expert locker-room coaching, the F L U Auto Delegates kicked off their first ball at the National Automotive Council (NAC) meeting in Detroit in June, 1934. Although some 20 or 30 locals had been using the NAC title for the past year, this was the first AFL called conference—and it hadn't been called willingly!

Some 150 delegates from 70 or 80 locals in a half dozen states took this opportunity to unload months of pent up wrath against AFL's procrastinating policies. The designs on dividing up the factory workers into the crafts; the almost total lack of men or money for an all out organizational drive; the autocratic and domineering attitude of the Executive Council; the refusal to help set up an Auto Workers National or International Union and many minor issues turned the conference into a red hot session.

The delegates were so incensed that they voted to throw all AFL Representatives out of the hall but Bill Green's powers of persuasion finally prevailed. The auto plants were too little organized to start their own International; GM, Ford, and Chrysler needed the expert attention of "professional AFL Organizers"; a full fledged organizing drive would soon be started; the new locals could set up an advisory board to help co-ordinate their efforts."

The delegates were disgusted and disgrunted but since most locals actually represented only a minor percentage of their plants they could do little else except to agree. Green appointed several members to the Advisory Board and the angry, disappointed delegates vowed to fight it out another day. Forrest Woods of 18310 was the Advisory Board Member for the Indiana District.

It seemed too little to be called even a hollow victory but the more sophisticated "advisors" reassured that it was a significant step. Said one old union veteran, "When a featherweight crawls into the ring with a heavyweight he isn't going for a knockout, he is trying to score some points. You guys made some points that you can't see now but they will prove mighty big in the days ahead."

Officials of Pioneer Days

The majority of the dedicated unionists who led the South Bend pioneers cannot be recognized in this account. Primitive and inadequate facilities allowed only rudimentary recording of names and events and many were never noted at all. Even the few records that survived through the pioneer period didn't survive the heavy insensitive hands of some of the later generations. An extra needed drawer of file space and a total lack of esthetic value sent priceless gems of history into the burning barrels.

For every name noted herein there were at least a dozen others who contributed equal, and often much greater services. Even the names of some Executive Board members and bargaining committeemen are missing from written record and human memory.

Local No. 18310 Officers 8-1-33 Through 12-31-34

President: *Ross McNabney
           **L. R. Richardson
           ***John Kolecki
           ****Russell J. Merrill
Vice President: Ben Moore
Executive Secretary: John H. Bartee
                     Alton Green
Recording Secretary: Alton Green
                     Jesse Harrell
Treasurer: Chester Ralston
           John Szabo, Jr.

Sergeant at Arms: **Vance Rzepka**
Leo Keister
Trustee: **Jesse Harrell**
Marley Hendricks
Clarence Keller
Joe Thilman
George Yarborough

(6 or 7 names of officers are missing)
Some 40 or 50 stewards and special committeemen are not listed.
*McNabney resigned after a few weeks to leave the shop and
**L. Richardson filled his term through December.
***John Kolecki was elected in December and resigned due to illness in March 1934.
****Russell Merrill was elected to replace Kolecki.

Local 13847 Officers 8-17-33 Through 8-3-35

President: ***William Hull**
***Carl Shipley**
Vice President: **Carl Shipley**
Virgil McGee
Financial Secretary: **Walter B. Saxton**
Treasurer: **Robert Hamilton**
Recording Secretary: **Felix Goron**
James R. Poland
Trustee: **Wilbur (Howdy) Wilcox**
H. O. Hurley
Executive Board: ****Sam Peckens**
James McEwan

Mack Foy
****Bob Hamilton**
Elmer Gollnick
H. A. Black
Chief Stewards:
Pete Ruppert
H. A. Black

*Hull resigned and was replaced by Shipley.
**Peckens resigned: **Hamilton replaced him.

CHAPTER 9

UAW'S FIRST CONVENTION

THE MOST positive action of the 1934 Conference of NAC was the resolve to hold a Constitutional Convention the following year. All around their circuit the Auto Workers built up their hopes for an effective organization that would give them a united front.

The Convention was called for mid-August 1935, at the Fort Shelby Hotel in Detroit. Some 148 plants in 14 states were represented but probably no more than 8 or 10 had a majority of signed up dues paying members. The majority status of both Local 18310 and Local 18347 was close to 90%. Local 18310 sent 10 delegates and Local 18347 sent 9. They were by far the largest Local Union Delegations in attendance.

There were a number of Locals not affiliated with AFL who came to see whether or not the proposed UAW was to their liking. The Press smelled a portentous event about to happen and were there in force.

AFL President Bill Green insisted that the new Union must accept his appointment Francis Dillon, AFL Staff Member, as President. His reasons were:

> No one among them had the skill, ability, or experience to handle such a responsible and trying job. An equally compelling reason, he asserted, was thet there was not enough money available to the new Locals to operate a National Union on their own.

The delegates protested but Green prevailed. However, he did concede to them on the selection of a Vice President and Secretary-Treasurer. They elected Ed Hall of Seaman's Body Plant in Milwaukee as Secretary-Treasurer, and Homer

Martin of the Kansas City Ford Plant as Vice President. The angry delegates served notice that "next year" they would elect all of their officers.

The old Federal Labor Union local numbers were dropped and new numbers issued. Local 18310 became Local #5 and Local 18347 became Local #9 of the United Automobile Workers of America! Why the two originals drew such high numbers is a riddle of history.

Winds of Change

By 1936 Industrial Unionism in South Bend was gaining many supporters, increasing its militancy, and making a marked impact economically, socially, and politically. There were however a few elements of society that looked upon this new force with dismay and foreboding. Politicians of both major parites, especially at county and municipal levels, assumed (quite correctly) that their private preserves were in danger. Liberal Democrats were pleased but the conservatives joined with the Republicans in a cold, hostile attitude of disapproval.

This attitude brought about a movement to attempt the formation of a Farmer-Labor Party. Some areas in Wisconsin and Minnesota had made such substantial gains through Farmer-Labor policies that it seemed worth a try.

An organizational convention was held in Indianapolis in October with the basic purpose of learning how well such a movement would be received.

Interest was not as widespread as hoped but the fervor of its supporters was great enough to help liberal Democrats convince their party that labor was too powerful to ignore. Like all politicians they had a sensitive feel for the Winds of Change!

Free Convention

Mounting pressure from the UAW Local Unions and from the liberal wing of AFL set the stage for UAW's first free convention. South Bend, the recognized center of the Auto Workers' movement, was chosen as the natural site, and Local No. 5's $58,000.00 treasury balance helped substantially to underwrite the expense.

With Local 5 and Local 9 as co-hosts, the convention started on April 27, 1936 — some two years and ten months after their time of genesis. Thirty-four charter members plus thirty-four months of hard work had been added up to make a lot of dreams come true. In addition to the several hundred delegates there were at least as many observers. Due to the skeletal condition of most locals, membership rolls and bank accounts, expense money was minimal but they "made do" with practice learned in the Big Depression. Some were house guests of local unionists and others slept four to eight men in a hotel room.

Walter Reuther brought the entire treasury of his local union, $5.00! He and four others slept in a one bed room as did dozens of others. The brilliant mind and articulate tongue of the greatest of all Labor Statesmen made a tremendous impression. Truly, destiny was smiling on UAW.

The AFL Old Guard saw its youngest and most precocious offspring cast off parental ties. Bill Green was there to officially cancel the parent union's administrationship and to give AFL's blessings to UAW's newly declared freedom. For their officers they elected Homer Martin as President, Wyndham Mortimer, Ed Hall and Walter Wells as Vice-Presidents, and George Addes as Secretary-Treasurer. By convention action "Board" members were elected from various regions to direct UAW efforts. Later this office was titled "Regional Director." Russell J. Merrill, president of Local 5, was elected to serve in the Indiana Region. Insufficient income prevented making all of the new jobs full time so most of the Board members had to retain their old jobs until the International's income improved.

Among the observers were many interested "shoppers" looking for an organization to match their ideals and needs. Some were from Federal Labor locals not yet affiliated with UAW; others came from Independent Unions with no AFL ties. They were so impressed that the majority merged their Locals with the new International within a short time after the convention. Also, among the observers were a number of professional Management-Labor Consultants. Their job was to weigh its potential power and estimate the impact of the new union upon the automobile industry. A consultant of long experience remarked to a Studebaker executive:

"Here is the Union with all of the potential power and drive that Business has always feared but if they keep those lofty ideals they won't last long in the AFL!"

An aging former coal miner of Local 5 prophesied: "in ten years we'll be a million strong; we'll have members from coast to coast—from Alaska to the Rio Grande!" One of the many fringe benefits of the broad gathering of workers was the inspiring enthusiasm that rubbed off on all concerned. Craft unionists openly wished that such spirit might be instilled in their unions' memberships. People in the shops who had held mixed feelings about the union now endorsed it fervently. Even the non union workers in many offices received some tandem benefits in wage raises granted by their employers to dampen a growing union consciousness.

CHAPTER 10

STATISTICS OF A NEW UNION

I N THE FIRST formal layout of UAW regions, Indiana and central and southern Illinois in 1937 were designated as Region 8. The Illinois portion ran north from the state line on the south to the northern borders of the following counties: Mercer, Henry, Bureau, LaSalle, Grundy, and Will.

Russell J. Merrill of Local 5 was the Regional Director. Headquarters were at 327 K. of P. Building, Indianapolis. Regional Councils (now the Auto Council) were set up to facilitate organizing and to maintain close liaison. The original officers of the Regional Council of Region 8:

President — Charles Lynch	Local 5
Vice President — Charles Schrock	Local 57
Financial Secretary — Tom Jeffers	Local 9
Recording Secretary — Clay Stinson	Local 265

Region 8 in 1937

Local	Location	Members	Local	Location	Members
5	South Bend	6078	315	Connersville	
9	South Bend	3027	340	Huntington	87
57	Ft. Wayne	383	370	New Castle	
143	Plymouth	37	371	New Castle	1025
144	South Bend	87	390	Connersville	
146	Anderson	900	411	New Albany	
151	Connersville	800	413	Richmond	400
152	Connersville	200	430	Richmond	
167	South Bend	1100	442	Indianapolis	
171	Alexandria	300	452	Venice, Illinois	
176	South Bend	213	458	Portland	
183	South Bend	446	459	Muncie	100

194	Ft. Wayne	100	478	Portland	
200	(no information)		484	Richmond	
224	South Bend	160	489	Muncie	400
226	Indianapolis	1000	492	Laporte	
265	Evansville	2900	494	Union City	200
267	Alexandria		495	Muncie	136
287	Muncie	1300	499	Muncie	200
292	Kokomo	300	518	Springfield, Illinois	
			530	Laporte	

(The data contained herein is from the records of Charles Lynch.) It is assumed that those locals without any membership listing were not yet affiliated with the Regional Council.

The Union Dollar

The division of $1.00 per month dues in 1937 (Local 5).

$.375   International per capita tax.

.02   Local CIO Council per capita tax.

.01   State CIO Council per capita tax.

.01   Regional Auto Council per capita tax.

.01   Labor Non-Partisan League Per capita tax.

.02   Local's Death Benefit Fund.

.05   Building Fund.

.05   Defense Fund.

.455   Local's General Fund

(From Lynch records).

UAW's First Three Conventions

No. 1 Detroit, August 26-31, 1935. There were 210 delegates reported to be representing 27,700 members. It was recorded that an additional 7,500 members were not represented. There were 148 locals from 14 states registered.

No. 2 South Bend, April 27 through May 2, 1936. There were 215 delegates representing 24,300 members registered. There were 151 locals from 14 states. The records show that 5300 members were not represented by delegates.

No. 3 Milwaukee, Wisconsin, August 17-23, 1937. Delegates from 256 locals represented 189,100 dues paying members.

Wage Journal of a Studebaker Assembler

Year	Hours Worked	Average Piece Work Rate	Total Earnings
1933	1290.5	$ .5233	$ 675.32
1934	1075.5	.7308	785.94
1935	1421.5	.7888	1121.10
1936	1674.5	.8978	1503.36
1937	1410.75	.9517	1342.55
1938	794.25	.9944	789.84
1939	1770.25	1.0045	1778.23

(From Charles Lynch's records of his own earnings).

International Union Income

	10-1-35 to 3-31-36	4-1-36 to 12-31-36	1-1-37 to 6-30-37
Per Capita	36,846.56	85,194.71	410,383.93
Education Fund	2,622.74	6,388.73	32,189.77
Initiation Fees	3,465.50	16,694.25	310,391.80
Reinstatement Fees	727.80	2,917.60	3,573.55
Supplies and Misc.	3,568.31	7,503.98	86,546.96
Organization Fund		14,280.15	13,419.19
Strike Donations	1,850.89	1,571.65	56,123.03

The 8 highest contributors 4-1-36 through 12-31-36

Local	3	Detroit	$ 5,589.25
Local	5	South Bend	18,330.96
Local	12 Amalgamated	Toledo, Ohio	17,960.82
Local	32	Cleveland, Ohio	9,522.41
Local	58	Racine, Wis.	2,741.52
Local	72	Kenosha, Wis.	7,355.17
Local	75	Racine, Wis.	9,989.02
Local	131	Norwood, Ohio	5,429.13

This represented 57% of UAW's total income for that 9 month period.

Ebb and Flow Economy
Membership Dues Paid to Local Number 5

	1936	1937
January	5526	5073
February	4669	7936
March	5281	4492
April	3569	8361
May	5580	7221
June	4399	4049
July	2254	7034
August	3249	3192
September	4661	6894
October	7340	9070
November	5026	3584
December	6032	4024

A Dream Comes True

One of its earliest acts as a free International Union was UAW's affiliation with the already momentum gathering Committee for Industrial Organization (CIO).

Substantial cash grants from the United Mine Workers, the Amalgamated Clothing Workers and some of the smaller Internationals provided the long needed money. A force of experienced and dedicated organizers provided by all CIO affiliates took on the job that Studebaker and Bendix pioneers had started agitating for in 1933. Rid at last of the grasping, jurisdiction crazy domination of the AFL craft union dictators, the hitherto handicapped organization of industry by industry could proceed. The South Bend pioneers turned again to local shops that jurisdictional claims had kept them from organizing earlier. New unions began to grow at amazing speed in the fertile fields tilled by CIO.

A Mini Boom

Studebaker car sales in early 1936 were so good that they hired a thousand new employees in August and September. These, with some fifty exceptions, were the first production workers hired since 1929's boom days. The greatest majority were young men who had never had a full time job before.

Local 5 and 9 members had been working forty or more hours per week since late 1935 and it was reflected in booming retail sales. Even the local Chamber of Commerce indirectly admitted that the new and dynamic industrial labor movement had been good for South Bend. Both locals pressed their managements for wage increases and contracts to protect the gains already won. Both companies however, had their "weather eyes" on Detroit, the main center of automobile production, and were reluctant to incur the wrath of the industry's giants.

CHAPTER 11

LOCAL 9 LEADS OFF

T HE FREEDOM of movement and the right to make constructive plans had a tremendous affect on the dynamic new union. Rid at last of the stifling influence of the AFL's Executive Committee, they began to do the things that had hitherto been forbidden. The militancy so long held captive came into full bloom all around the automobile circuit. Tired of the industry's flouting of the Wagner Act (passed in 1935) UAW prepared for a massive all-out movement to win economic justice. Local 9, fed up with the tactics of the Bendix Corporation, led off with a then unknown new strategy, **the sit down strike.** Later on there were larger and longer strikes but none created as much interest or fired the imagination like the one at Bendix.

It was a well organized manuever and its execution was timed for the Company's busiest season. The tight little world of the Auto Barons shook to its gold plated foundation!

Company threats to starve out the strikers were defeated by the Union's strategy of sending in food by U.S. mail. Freeze-out threats were foiled by public opinion and the fear of ruining their own equipment. Threats of force were dampened by Local 5's 7000-member warning "just let them try it". Equally ineffective were company threats dinned continuously over the shop speaker system to get out or face the indefinite closing of the plant. After six days Management saw the Union's determination growing rather than diminishing and pushed hard by their customers, they finally gave in. Some three years of accumulated Union demands were the price of settlement. Basically the main points were:

1. All employees must be returned to work with full seniority.
2. The Company Union must be eliminated—Local 9 to be the only bargaining agent.
3. A Board of Review to act on complaints must be established.
4. A 1-day notice to be given before all lay offs.
5. 2 hours call-in pay when no work was available.

Throughout the industrial unions of the country the impact of Local 9's victory was a powerful stimulus. CIO took in a stature in the eyes of American workers that AFL had never been able to inspire. UAW was at last on the long hard road to success!

Local 5's First Contract

In early 1937 while the sit down strikers struggled valiantly in Detroit, Local No. 5 succeeded in getting the Studebaker Corporation into serious contract negotiations. It started out to be a marathon endurance contest, but a battle wise union leadership was never dissuaded from its objective.

Studebaker wage rates and the company policy on employee remuneration in general were archaic and often chaotic. More than 85 years of ingrown habits had set up some glaring inequities and cumbersome procedure.

There were hundreds of job titles but they failed to adequately describe the tasks. The same job might have a half dozen titles and often three or four different pay rates in various areas of the plants. There were five different rates for janitors, three for spot welders, four for punch press, etc.

The relative value of jobs was seldom reflected in an equitable manner. Millwrights in some instances ranked above tool makers. Some rates were as much as twenty percent lower than comparable jobs in other divisions. Even Management agreed that it was a mess!

All attempts of the Union to get joint cooperation in straightening out the mess were unavailing so a union committee took on the job. After months of exhaustive study and consulting with workers in every category, the Committee presented their proposals to Management. When the contract was finally consumated the Committee's wage structure was adopted almost verbatim.

Finally on May 21, 1937 the long awaited contract was won. Just forty-six months from the date of being chartered! It was indeed a time for celebration, and celebrate we did! For that early period the contract provided some amazing benefits. A modernized wage system; plant wide seniority; a fast acting grievance procedure; ten percent night shift premium, time and one-half for over eight hours a day and forty hours per week; vacation pay and many other benefits that came years later to most new unions. One unique feature was the right to open the contract by giving a 60-day notice at any time. This provision was carried for 17 years without abuse by either party.

When the new unionists first joined AFL one of their first desires was to learn about the history of the Labor Movement. Public schools had taught very little about unions and even that was biased and propagandized. News media said few good things about Labor because their big advertisers wouldn't approve. The public libraries in the South Bend area had few informative books on unions because most donors were definitely not pro-union. While the AFL in South Bend had very little literature a few of the affiliates did, and many studious individual union members were helpful. Before they owned a desk or typewriter Local 18310 started gathering bits and pieces of educational material most of which was purchased by individual members. When they moved to 919 South Michigan Street there already was the nucleus of a good labor library. Eventually a large room was filled with books both old and current, and a librarian was hired. This became a study and lecture center doing labor, political and economic research and conducting information classes long before most of the CIO international Unions had any facilities at all for educational programs.

The two hundred year old history of the ups and downs, the short lived victories and crushing defeats of American labor efforts taught many needed lessons. The perfidy, ruthlessness, and brutal tyranny of the over-lords of American industry and commerce against their employees was a revelation that had long needed to be made. Many union members learned for the first time how badly workers were being exploited.

Labors experiences in foreign lands taught many lessons on what to do and, often more important, what not to do. Many techniques either unknown or unused by the AFL, were beneficial to the fledging Auto Workers.

CHAPTER 12

YEARS OF TURBULENCE

BEFORE UAW had been a free union for two years trouble from within threatened to wreck the new organization. Very early in 1938 the evidence was all too clear that their choice of President Martin had been unwise. His eloquence from the podium was not reflected either at the bargaining table or in handling the affairs of the Union. He ignited disunity among other officers and fed the fires with peevish cirticism to cover his own ineffectiveness. His attempts at back-door agreements with some of the big Auto Companies was the final straw.

The South Bend pioneers watched with sadness and dismay but all of the numerous efforts to conciliate were fruitless. Homer Martin had become so snarled in the schemes of the small clique of self seeking exploiters advising him that he was totally incapable of listening to good advice. The emissaries of Locals 5 and 9 sadly reported back to their Local Unions that any patching up of relations was hopeless. Nothing less than a complete overhaul could save the UAW from disaster.

Consultations was held with John L. Lewis, Phillip Murray, David Dubinsky, Sidney Hillman and other prominent union leaders. All realized the gravity of the problem and had already been trying to reconcile the differences involved. They agreed to try again but warned the South Bend leaders that the chances of reaching a real settlement were almost nil.

It was very probable, they counseled, that a split between the Martin forces and his opponents might in the long run be the best solution. It was their opinion that Homer Martin with his erratic and unpredictable ways might decide to wreck UAW rather than agree to work with its more able leaders. They pointed out that the entire CIO movement in the field of industrial organizing depended upon the successful progress of UAW. In addition to setting a shining example of how well factory workers unions could do for their members, it was living proof that no employer was too big to be organized.

Sydney Hillman and Phillip Murray did intervene and succeeded in patching up a temporary truce. This lasted in a troubled and nebulous state until the end of the year. The final blow up came in January of 1939 when Martin suspended fifteen members of the Executive Board and the Board countered by impeaching Martin.

The Unity Group led by Walter Reuther, Wyndham Mortimer and George Addes represented well over 80 percent of the UAW members. Martin's Progressive group however had control of the International Treasury, thus leaving his opponents with no money for salaries or expenses. It was a time of sorrow and dismay for the industrial workers in America.

The Unity faction moved fast and effectively to avoid further catastrophe, with Local 5 and several others supplying stop gap funds, a convention was called for March at Cleveland, Ohio. Martin called his own convention in Detroit and claimed he had 90 percent of the members behind him. CIO officials learned that Martin was preparing to seize all of the larger treasuries in the Locals that supported the Unity faction. Most of the Locals took fast action to save their funds. Local 5 hid its $70,000 in a half dozen safe depositories in the small towns around South Bend. The Martin forces took court action to grab the Local 9 treasury but were not successful.

The total in loans and outright grants from Local 5 to the Unity faction was well in excess of $25,000.00. The Cleveland convention drew delegates from all but a handful of UAW Locals. R. J. Thomas was elected President. George Addes was re-elected Secretary-Treasurer and UAW-CIO was back on the main track again.

Homer Martin led his hapless little minority back into the AFL. His ineptitude as a leader coupled with AFL's backward philosophy kept the splinter group in a sorry state. Even after he was forced out of leadership the UAW-AFL couldn't gain momentum enough to do a good job.

The reorganization of UAW at the 1939 convention proved out to be one of its best ventures. By mid 1940 the two original locals of South Bend had so many sister locals around the country that few people could identify all of them. The center of industrial unionism had gravitated to Detroit and was growing at an amazing rate under an enlightened leadership.

The names of CIO and UAW were becoming famous world wide for their exploits in organizing the "unorganizable." The eventual organization of the "one man empire" of Henry Ford was, in almost everybody's opinion, only a matter of time.

Recession

In the late fall of 1937 the hitherto accelerating economy began to slow down. The ordinary signs of a business slump that had always before preceded the all too frequent "panics", were absent. Some business spokesmen blamed it on the Union's wage demands and Roosevelt's "Socialistic" policies.

The columnists who slavishly portrayed the reactions of their Big Business sponsors berated the New Deal, the CIO, and everyone else with any liberal leaning.

Economists for the Federal and many state Governments labeled it as a man made "recession." The long time rulers of America's economy were trying to regain their old time control. Layoffs and dole lines came back but now there was a difference. There were no runs on the banks because deposit insurance had eliminated that evil. The PWA, WPA and CCC moved fast to provide stop-gap employment for the unemployed. Food, clothing, fuel and utilities for the destitute were more plentiful, of better quality and the stigma of charity was gone.

Older Studebaker employees shared employment with their newly hired fellow employees until their unemployment compensation became available in January of 1938. When the work hours dropped to 12 and 16 hours per week the Union negotiated to work every other week. This allowed three to four days of work one week and $15 unemployment benefits the next. It was indeed a far cry from the Hoover days! The recession faded away after about ten months, but it had demonstrated that President Roosevelt's depression antidotes really worked.

CHAPTER **13**

THE FIRST FIVE YEARS

T HE FIRST TWO and a quarter pages of President Lewis' report to CIO's initial constitutional convention tells one of the most unique success stories in all of history. The story began in the fall of 1933 when Federal Labor Unions 18310 and 18347 rebelled against AFL's piracy habits.

Report of Chairman John L. Lewis
Of the Committee for Industrial Organizations

Pittsburgh, Pa., November 14, 1938.

To the Officers and Delegates of the First Constitutional Convention of the Committee for Industrial Organizations, Greetings:

This is an historic occasion. Today we fit the rooftree in a mighty new house of labor. Where three years ago there was only an idea in the minds of a few men, there now stands a structure as solidly built as if of stone and steel.

This is an occasion for rejoicing among the proponents of advancing democracy, among men of good will.

It is an occasion for gloom only among those to whom real democracy means the loss of their excess privileges, among those who seek the subjection of the common people.

The proponents of democracy in many lands are fighting a losing battle against forces of anti-democracy and political immorality. In many countries tyranny has supplanted freedom. More and more each day our nation looms as the guardian of human liberty and justice. It is not an easy trusteeship.

Our people in this movement know how hard it is to preserve their rights and their liberty — even within democracy. They have battled against violence, brutality and calumny. The forces of public order have been perverted against them. And yet our people have not faltered in their conviction that they have rights which must not be destroyed.

The agencies of public information have boiled with jeremiads against the Committee for Industrial Organization. On no other occasion of modern times has the American ideal of free press been so sullied. The loyalty of the members and friends of the CIO through these storms of falsity shows again that American people will not be misled by cynical untruths and bitter misrepresentations.

There are those who misunderstand us, our aims and our methods; there are some who have been misled about us through lack of knowledge and perception. From them we seek only what is the right of every American — a fair judgment upon the facts. We are firm in the conviction that such a judgment can only be that our movement must grow ever stronger if democracy is to continue to survive.

The CIO has brought body and substance to the idea of progressive democracy and economic stability. It has finally assumed in our nation that economic and political position which rightly belongs to a labor movement. The program of the CIO has a twofold purpose. The first is to bring security and liberty to those who work for their living. In achieving this it is our conviction that we implement the second purpose, the creation of economic and social stability. It is only upon such economic stability that a lasting democratic form of government can exist. In the political field we seek to advance these economic aims and to help preserve the liberty necessary to attain them.

To millions, because of this movement, the word "liberty" has acquired new meaning. Often those who seek only license for their plundering, cry "liberty". In the guise of this old American ideal, men of vast economic domain would destroy what little remains to those who toil. The liberty we seek is different. It is liberty for common people — freedom from economic bondage, freedom from the oppressions of the vast bureaucracies of great corporations, freedom to regain again some human initiative, freedom that arises from economic security and human self-respect.

No people know better than the workers in this great industrial city how those aims of the CIO are translated into the facts of daily life. Here once was a center of economic oppression. Here now is rising a new structure of industrial peace and liberty.

We are here to dedicate a labor movement, a labor movement born of economic necessity, impelled by the unquenchable desire to better the lot of fellow men, and led onward by the just principles upon which our nation was founded. In it lies the hope of America.

The first constitutional convention of the Committee for Industrial Organization represents the coming of age of a movement whose rapid rise and substantial achievements in less than three years, are without parallel in labor history.

The small committee of eight union presidents which first met in the fall of 1935 to promote industrial organization in the mass-production industries, has been transformed in this period into a great new labor movement, representing more than four million organized workers.

The committee started its work with the intention of bringing the unorganized mass-production workers into the American Federation of Labor. But it was frustrated in this purpose by the arbitrary action of the Executive Council of the AFL, which drove the CIO unions out of the Federation in September, 1936, for pursuing their constructive task of industrial organization.

This action left the CIO unions no other recourse but to continue their organizing activities outside the AFL.

Once freed from the incubus of the craft bureaucracy which had previously strangled all genuine attempts to spread union organization to the millions of unorganized, the CIO was able to release energies and enthusiasm which had not been able to find expression before. As a result, millions of workers joined the ranks of union labor, once they were assured that a new and more progressive movement had arisen which would assure them their full rights to unite in powerful industrial unions covering all workers in their respective industries.

In the two years that have followed the expulsion of the CIO unions from the AFL, the whole structure of the Committee for Industrial Organization has been transformed from that of an organizing committee to a congress of scores of industrial unions, representing a majority of the organized workers in our country.

Many new industrial unions have been granted affiliation with the CIO and hundreds of Local Industrial Unions have been chartered. In addition, the local and district units of the CIO unions have combined in their various states and cities to set up Industrial Union Councils as the democratic expression of the whole movement in the respective states and localities.

This convention has been called as the culminating step in completing the organizational structure of our movement and to establish the CIO on a permanent and democratic basis, as the representative central body of all the affiliated unions.

CHAPTER 14

PARASITES

IN SOME OF THE larger centers Communism's interest in the new Industrial Unions became evident in early 1934. The first manifestations in South Bend were in 1935 but mid-1936 was the earliest that they became active enough to be identified.

The leaders of Locals 5 and 9 soon found they had a new and formidable adversary with an unfamiliar bag of tricks.

What they lacked in logic they made up with fervent rhetoric and their lack in numbers was made up by mobility, perseverance and a burning dedication to their Marxist cause. Their first step strategy was to ingratiate themselves with the union leadership and this was indeed a deadly and effective technique. No task was too rough—they'd do it with a smile. Heat, cold, rain or snow never deterred them and their greatest glory was to be seen at picket lines when the "action was on." UAW's more sophisticated friends in the needle trades (Amalgamated Clothing, Ladies Garment and Textile Unions) warned that to get involved with Communism was like getting hooked on dope—easy and pleasant to get into but hard to "kick." They had their initiation in the early 1920's and knew what was behind those friendly, eager to please tactics.

Their basic hard core operatives were highly trained, clever and masters in the art of hooking shock troops for their use. The unwary suckers were almost always hooked securely before they learned who the "fishermen" really were. They generally found it easier and safer to stay in than to get out.

The recruits were for the most part a motley and pitiable lot. Malcontents and misfits — mentally and psychologically slanted against society — made up the majority of the converts.

There were, however, some well educated and otherwise intelligent individuals caught up in the nets of the "Red Fishermen." Some were short-sighted idealists seeking a fast outlet for their fervor while others were ambitious opportunists looking for a ladder to success.

Like birds with lice and dogs with fleas, the new unions had acquired their parasites. They would have to endure them until an eradicator could be developed but no one knew then what a long and hectic process that was to be!

Hitler's evil alliance with the Soviet Union and his ruthless brutality against Poland had shocked and outraged the free world. Out of it grew some of the unanswerable enigmas of the Communist doctrine. The missionaries of the hammer and sickle cult in South Bend had preached long and loud on the sins and iniquities of the Fascists and Nazis. They were an abomination to mankind, the antithesis of everything good. America's only salvation was for the workers to unify under the banner of that great workers' republic, the Soviet Union. No other course could save the world from Hitler and Mussolini!

Then out of a clear sky Stalin signed that fateful non-aggression pact with Hitler. With their world in a shambles around them, with all their preachments discredited, the peddlers of Communism were only temporarily stunned. Within a few weeks they had developed new arguments to support their old doctrines. "This, they preached, "was Europe's war and it must be left to the Europeans to settle. The United States needed all of its money and resources at home. France and Great Britain didn't deserve, and mustn't have, any help from America."

Some phase or other of this doctrine of the Marxists bedeviled Local Union membership meetings, council meeting and conferences in South Bend until the exasperated UAW members started unmasking them. The resulting debates were often entertaining, always heated, and never dull!

Several useful purposes were accomplished by the hassles. The anti-red debaters developed great expertise, Commies and their sympathizers were identified; the Stalin-Hitler combine was kept always in focus and pro French and pro British adherents multiplied.

Then in June of 1941 Hitler without warning attacked Russia, and the American hammer and sickle salesmen were caught in the middle again. With faces as red as their ideologies they reversed their preaching in mid air. "Europe was the mother land of America — it must not be allowed to fall before the savages of the Third Reich." "Americans should forego their right to overtime pay — give up the 8-hour day — work from dawn till dark to defeat the Nazi and Fascist monsters."

How the same individuals could so slavishly ape the Communist line through the twisting, turning and reversing of those days was beyond comprehension. In the long run it proved to be a valuable education for the South Bend Unions' anti-red shock troops. After Pearl Harbor when the U.S. unavoidably became involved in the war on the same side as the Soviet Union, the parasites grew very bold.

When Bendix and Studebaker doubled, then tripled their work forces to build war equipment the Commies came in numbers. Almost immediately they showed their real intentions by insolently trying to wrest control of the Local Unions from the officers. The earlier training on Communist tactics stood the Locals in good stead.

Directly after the end of World War II the Communists turned on all of their resources to seize control of CIO. It was a many faceted war of subversion, seduction, perfidy, propaganda, and often, violence. Their bag of tricks seemed bottomless. The vital, new labor organization was, to the Commies, a prize beyond compare.

Under the able and brilliant leadership of Walter Reuther, UAW's battle scarred veterans of many conflicts took on the "Red Menace". The final defeat of the Marxists greatest drive came in 1949 at the CIO Convention in Cleveland. Under Reuther's expert and courageous generalship, one of American Labor's greatest threats was overcome. The chief strategists of South Bend's "anti-Red" forces were there to celebrate and rejoice.

Saga of Jurisdiction

The right of a single national or international union to represent all of the employees in a specific plant or industry was the hottest of inter-union issues in the mid-1930's. The very mention of the "industrial union" in Old Guard circles was sacrilege and always good for a long harangue on its evils and shortcomings. The running debate was picked up by the press and they, along with various employer associations joined in the vilification of the "plant wide" union.

From the time of the new unionists first knowledge of AFL intentions (November 1933) until the final schism in the fall of 1936 a running battle ensued. AFL's golden opportunity to parlay its 3 and a half million members into 18 or 20 million was lost forever in its blind opposition to change.

The International Association of Machinists (IAM) was the spearhead in the plot to slice up the new factory unions. If their try at it worked many others were waiting in the wings!

An early dialogue between an auto worker and an IAM official went something like this:

"How many Studebaker workers do the Machinists claim?"

"Everyone that works in the machine shops."

"What do you mean by machine shop? Are you talking about the tool and die makers or do you claim others too?"

"Oh, we are entitled to a lot more than those. Millwrights, machine repairmen, precision inspectors, in fact, all of the skilled people around machines."

"How about production workers on machines?"

"We really have jurisdiction over all machine operating employees."

"Does that include welding and riveting, and sewing machines?"

"Well—I don't know about those, particularly the sewing machines!"

"If the IAM gets the machinists, what other unions will want their cut?"

"Up to now, we are the only ones."

"But, could it happen later—that is if you get by with it? What about the Plumbers, the Electricians, the Carpenters, etc. and maybe even the Laborers?"

"Well—that's up to the Executive Committee of AFL but, I don't think they would approve the Laborers!"

"Suppose we disagree with the Executive Committee and keep all of our workers? Suppose the delegates at the next convention order us to comply and we refuse?"

"Well—unions that refuse to follow policy are sometimes suspended!"

At first it all sounded almost too preposterous for belief but a year later (October 1934) at the San Francisco Convention of AFL all doubts ended. A resolution was introduced and passed overwhelmingly to give IAM jurisdiction over all of the skilled workers connected in anyway with the Machinists' trades.

They did, however, back away from demanding control over production machine operators.

Several powerful AFL affiliates opposed the Machinists' demands on the grounds that it was unfair and would discourage factory workers from organizing. Their arguments were snowed under by the delegates under the control of the Old Guard majority on the Executive Council. The handful of green and penniless auto delegates had lost their battle but had gained some powerful and resourceful allies.

The reactions to the San Francisco decision were many and varied, depending upon the groups being affected. Most employers were pleased because it looked like a windfall "union stopper" for them. Among the embryo groups in thousands of factories just starting to talk about union there was dismay and confusion.

The liberal unions in AFL began talking about action as serious as secession if such became necessary.

The auto locals in South Bend dedicated themselves to the formation of a National or International Union for auto and parts plant employees before another year should pass. There would be no slicing away of any segments!

The combined pressure from the fired-up new locals and the progressive elements among the older AFL unions finally prevailed. A Convention of Auto Workers was called in August of 1935 at the Fort Shelby Hotel in Detroit.

At UAW's 1935 Convention in Detroit, the issue of inter-union piracy was given a full airing. Even though there were many opinions on other issues, there couldn't have been more emphatic unity against inter-union cannibalism.

The Auto Delegates pointed out that many of them had been approached by farm implement and aircraft workers who wanted to organize. Their greatest deterrent was fear of AFL splitting them into splinter groups in their plants. It was suggested that the Auto Union be allowed to invite agricultural and aviation equipment workers to join them. AFL's answer was that they had better organize Auto first and leave the other industries alone.

In the matter of jurisdiction, the new UAW was to include all auto employees except the machinists!

The next big jurisdictional battle came at the Atlantic City AFL Convention in October, 1935. The rights of industrial unions to represent all of their plant workers were eloquently and ably defended but the opponents had the votes.

The Machinists right to invade the Auto Workers ranks was retained but it was a costly victory. With the AFL liberals already moving rapidly towards a massive drive to organize factories in every industry the Old Guard had in effect repudiated the very principle of industrial unionism.

The Convention did, however, allow the formation of the Committee that later became the Committee for Industrial Organization (CIO). The new UAW had lost another skirmish but won its big battle.

South Bend organizing picked up impetus from the launching of CIO and Locals 5 and 9 acquired some new allies from the local shops.

There were a few probing attempts from the Machinists to implement their "rights" to raid but they were repulsed.

The next big event in the war on jurisdiction came in April 1936 at the UAW Convention at the Indiana Club in South Bend.

Beefed up by thousands of new members and the formidable support of CIO the new International asserted its rights. It would represent all of its plant employees including the Machinists! It would elect all of its officers and would no longer tolerate Old Guard domination!

This rebellion by UAW and the increasing momentum of the industrial union movement with CIO alarmed the Old Guard. Seemingly incapable of constructive action they reacted by the Executive Committee suspending all of CIO from their ranks. This occurred in September 1936 and was sustained by the AFL Convention in November.

Thus ended some three years of what the South Benders called "stifling control" and opened up the road to democratic unionism.

It Wasn't Easy

One of the greatest fallacies of contemporary opinion is that organizing unions in the mid 1930s and early 40s was generally rather easy. Many seem to believe that after GM and Chrysler were won the only tough one left was Ford. Nothing could be farther from the truth. Man for man hundreds of managements of small and medium size plants — 100 to 1000 employees — resisted with all of the ruthlessness and vigor of the big ones.

It wasn't until late in 1938 that the Wagner Act was finally accepted by employers as a law of the land. Before then the whole combine of anti-union — anti-New Deal forces declared it was unconstitutional, un-American and just had to be illegal. When the Act finally passed the Supreme Court test employer resistance never faltered — they merely changed strategy and modified their tactics.

In plant after plant in South Bend employees would build substantial union majorities and demand recognition only to be met with hostile refusal. From the first signs of organizing activity managements turned on the heat and used every union-busting technique that they thought would be effective. Professional union smashers provided the guidance and frequently the man power.

Their most devastating tactic was to maneuver an unprepared group into an ill considered strike. Then would follow some cleverly engineered violence on the picket lines to turn public opinion against the workers while more subtle tactics were prepared. Next would come the midnight house calls with shouted obscenities and vile threats or phone calls with slanderous accusations.

Refusal of credit, pressure from doctors and dentists to pay up and whispering campaigns about certain men's alleged misdeeds were favorite tricks. Back to work movements came as soon as the professional strike breakers had prepared the proper mood.

It took a long time and lots of bruises before the new comers to the industrial labor movement learned to beat the goons at their own game.

Oliver employees became the first victims in the winter of 1934-1935. They had at least two thirds of the workers signed up for the Union but when the goons and the creditors got through their majority was gone.

Singer workers were next in the winter of 1935-1936 even though their majority was 4 to 1.

In March of 1936 the Torrington employees with something like a 2 to 1 majority went the same hard route after a month of heroic but futile struggles.

Almost every Union in South Bend helped substantially with men and money in every one of these examples, but they still couldn't win. All of the shops were put on the "must win" list and the next time around they didn't lose. Organizing was not easier in the early days but the rank and file members of almost all locals did come out to help!

CHAPTER **15**

WORLD WAR II BEGINS

W HEN THE nation entered World War II the vital new Industrial Labor movement came forward with every source at its command. CIO's eight and a half years of experience in organizing and mobilizing stood the Country in good stead as it dropped its peaceful pursuits and turned to an all out war footing.

Labor leaders were there when new agencies had to be formed, work forces mobilized, rations systems devised or any other place where their skill and expertise could be used.

In South Bend the change from civilian to war production caused vast disruption and unemployment for the first six to eight months. One of the Unions' functions was to find employment in war plants for the laid off workers, and because of this effort thousands of people benefitted. In other areas where few or no unions existed unemployment and confusion about what to do became serious problems.

The Bendix Aircraft Division was already heavily involved in producing military plane equipment before the war began. Within a couple of months after Pearl Harbor it was bursting at the seams and putting up new buildings at top speed. The work force grew as fast as building capacity would allow.

Torrington, with its high demand machine tool products, also grew at a phenomenal rate. Workers in most of the other South Bend plants sought jobs elsewhere until their shops could tool for war work.

Studebaker was in the process of building a 21-acre plant for airplane engine production in South Bend, plus a 14-acre plant in Chicago, and a 10-acre facility in Fort Wayne. None of these were ready when the war started, but within a few months the first machines were turning.

Already producing a few small military trucks the operation was stepped up to maximum capacity as they prepared to move to larger facilities. These were to be the former passenger car lines that stood idle since a sad work force had watched the last car roll by in February of 1942.

No Strike Pledge

Very soon after the Nation started to gear up for war work talk started about the need for Organized Labor to give up its right to strike for the duration of the conflict. Big Business on the extreme right and communists and their fellow travelers on the extreme left, teamed up in favor!

Many sincere labor people felt that despite the danger of exploitation from union-hating employers, the pledge ought to be made. Others contended that Labor had proven itself much more responsible than Management, and that the workers' patriotism was a sufficient guarantee.

Some of the South Bend locals signed; others did not, but there were no major strikes. The "pledge" became a very sore point before the war ended. A few short-sighted employers took advantage of the moratorium and went back to their old pre-union practice but at war's end the Unions evened the accounts.

New Unionists

By the first anniversary of the war most of the UAW shops in South Bend were in war production and accelerating their output. Laid off employees were back and new ones were being hired.

The war time new hires came from many walks of life. Personnel from nonessential shops, offices, and stores moved into the war jobs. Thousands of women were hired for work that women had never performed before. At Studebaker more than 60 percent of the nearly 3000 women were either mothers, wives, or sweethearts of men in the military service.

Very few of the newly hired had ever belonged to, or knew much about unions, and quite naturally there were some reservations on the subject. The teachings of the 1930s hadn't been forgotten and these new employees soon became loyal and enthusiastic union members.

Unions Served Where Needed

UAW people served on Draft Boards, Ration Boards, the War Labor Board and in many other capacities. They put on war bond drives and union members bought many millions of dollars worth.

Blood donors sent vast quantities to the wounded. Many joint Union-Management Committees teamed up to do everything possible to help the service men at the front, in camp, and at the hospitals.

One of Local 5's many projects was at the Wakeman Hospital located in Camp Atterbury south of Indianapolis. It was started up around the mid-point of the war mainly to perform plastic surgery and to treat the victims of battle fatigue.

A relative visiting a patient there reported that the hospital personnel had been unable to procure many sorely needed supplies due to war time shortages. Even such common items as canes, crutches, and wheel chairs seemed to be hard to get.

A small committee from the Local visited the hospital and reported back. The facility was just getting started and needed a long list of items for therapy and recreation that were months away on waiting lists. Some of their wants had been deemed to be out of the question and unobtainable.

The membership voted to set up a committee and to start immediately on a program to supply the needed items including the "unobtainables". Plant collection of money and the necessary supplies, wherever possible, was authorized.

The project turned out to be a long term campaign that lasted until every want was filled. Truck loads of supplies plus express and mail order deliveries started flowing to the hospital.

Canes, crutches, walkers, and wheel chairs came out of attics, basements, and garages. Musical instruments by the hundred from harmonicas to a piano were obtained. Some were purchased new but most came as donations from union members and their friends. Some 50 new and reconditioned bicycles and 40 home work shop machine tools were obtained. These and some $2000.00 worth of gold and silver wire and fine leather had been on the "unobtainable" list.

Everything that was possible to obtain (See photos on page 57) that would aid in therapy, provide entertainment, or aid in education was provided. The unanimous sentiment was "We only wish we could do more."

CONCLUSION

The period involved in this brief profile will no doubt be covered by future and more competent historians. It will be listed as the era when the working men and women of America came into their own. The characters of these pages symbolize that great American movement.

The seeds of industrial labor revolution found South Bend to be a fertile ground at the right season for its genesis. The answer to a long quest for justice had at last been found.

Its benefits to so many are not the final result but an opening door to the future. The generations of today and tomorrow have inherited the tools to help build a better world.

May they use them wisely.